transform.

be resilient.

The Major Brands in Germany 2023

recreate. transform. be resilient.

Published by Lutz Dietzold for the German Design Council

with contributions from Annalena Baerbock, Lutz Dietzold, Dr. Robert Habeck, Mike Richter, and Isabelle Vérilhac

Rat für Formgebung
German Design Council

CALLWEY

Contents

Good design makes brands strong ...

... and companies successful.

PROF. MIKE RICHTER

Dr. Robert Habeck

FEDERAL MINISTER FOR ECONOMIC AFFAIRS AND CLIMATE ACTION

Greeting

Federal Ministry
for Economic Affairs
and Climate Action

An idea, however important or progressive it may be, will only become a breakthrough idea if it first becomes an attractive product. In the process of turning the idea into reality, product design is not just embellishment, but an important factor for the success of the product on the market. Design is not only about creating beautiful forms, but also about providing answers to the challenges of our time, updating current designs and making technical achievements accessible to the general public. This is especially true in times when innovations are needed at an ever-increasing pace to meet current social and environmental challenges.

We in Germany can be proud of the long and successful history of German design, of the industry's ability to turn forward-looking ideas that only existed in designers' heads or sketches into reality. The "Made in Germany" brand serves as a quality label for pioneering product innovations in almost all industries worldwide. We owe this in large part to the ingenuity and foresight of our designers. They know how to shape economic and social developments across cultural barriers in

a way that enthuses people. As creative minds and design creators, you know that attention to detail even in the smaller aspects of a product's design has a decisive influence on how successful the product will be. It is often the ideas of designers that make products and services particularly competitive.

I congratulate the German Design Council on your many years of successful work and wish you an avid readership for the anniversary publication "The Major Brands in Germany – recreate. transform. be resilient" that will be inspired by it and will work creatively to help shape our future.

Dr. Robert Habeck
Federal Minister for Economic Affairs and Climate Action

Annalena Baerbock

FEDERAL MINISTER FOR FOREIGN AFFAIRS,

Greeting

 Federal Foreign Office

The Russian war of aggression marks a watershed for our country's security policy. But it is also helping to catapult the German economic model into a new era. As an exporting nation, we remain committed to globalisation, openness and connectivity. At the same time, though, we recognise what many here have long ignored: interdependence also involves risks; trade is not necessarily followed by democratic change; business contacts need a level playing field if they are to be fair to all. And if we do not invest massively in innovations for the energy transition and digitalisation today, then others will overtake us in the global economy of tomorrow.

That is why the Federal Government is doing everything possible to ensure that the German and European economies remain the foundation of our prosperity. By hugely ramping up the energy transition – and ending our dependence on fossil energy from Russia. By investing in the digital transformation and key technologies. By making our supply chains more resilient and diversifying our business contacts. And by shaping our trade relations in line with our values – not least because our own companies benefit if, for example, no products of forced labour are sold in the European internal market.

This shift is being led by Germany's companies themselves – because they are responsible for shaping and driving it. Once again they, and the major German brands in particular, have an opportunity to demonstrate their innovative energy and their dynamism. From DAX-listed companies and SMEs to small start-ups, German businesses set global standards for sustainability and new technologies, thanks in no small measure to their close cooperation with our country's universities and research institutions. The prestige enjoyed by German products around the world is a crucial factor in Germany's positive image abroad. Our foreign policy can build on this. Equally, German business can continue to count on our support.

Yours sincerely,
Annalena Baerbock, MdB
Federal Minister for Foreign Affairs

13

ESSAYS
recreate. transform.
be resilient.

Good design makes brands strong and companies successful

PROF. MIKE RICHTER
PRESIDENT OF THE GERMAN DESIGN COUNCIL

Following this conviction, and with great foresight, the German Design Council was initiated in 1953 by the German Bundestag, endowed by German industry, with the aim of strengthening design as an economic factor. Today, the German Design Council is part of the global design community and, as "Germany's design authority," stands for a holistic concept of design that encompasses cultural as well as economic and ecological values. And these values, for all their constancy, are also subject to change.

It is becoming apparent that in the future, more than at any other time, concepts for a world that is not only ecologically but also socially more sustainable will have the best chances for economic success, since consumers' expectations of responsibly manufactured products are growing. And the legislative power will also impose the necessary guard rails on economic activity for the responsible use of resources and energy. Irrespective of this, we as entrepreneurs have a clear responsibility to lead the way, and this responsibility has intensified to a large extent in design.

Therefore, the German Design Council promotes research and innovation as well as its transfer into practical application for society and business. From a design perspective, we look at the full range of possible innovations, including economic, technological, ecological, social, and digital innovations in particular.

Alongside the megatopics of digital transformation and the energy turnaround, the topic of sustainability remains at the top of the agenda. The German Design Council addresses these megatopics with a practical range of events, conferences, seminars, workshops and concepts for effective communication of design competence. With trend and theme studies as well as brand and design audits, we support and advise companies of all sizes in all questions of brand, innovation and design.

With our awards, we provide motivation, support change processes, reward courage and foresight, and provide inspiration and positive guiding principles for companies that are perhaps only at the beginning of their transformation.

Design talents are engines of transformation.

In this context, the topic of promoting young talent also plays an important role, as design talents are engines of further development and transformation and therefore not only important for the innovative capacity of established companies, but also an essential part of the start-up culture of today and the brands of tomorrow.

For this reason, the German Design Council has always promoted and supported young designers with various projects and initiatives: as one of the world's leading competence centers for communication and knowledge transfer, we open up networks to newcomers and ensure public awareness of their work with competitions for young designers, such as the "German Design Award Newcomer" or the "German Design Graduates" platform

In this way, the German Design Council promotes the ideas of the young design generation and brings their perspective into companies. Incidentally, in 1969, industrial designer Hartmut Esslinger received the first newcomer award presented by the German Design Council. It opened the first doors for him on his journey, which led to one of many high points in the 1980s, when the first Apple Macintosh design language was developed together with Steve Jobs. Part of his success story as a designer was to work exclusively for companies that made design a top priority.

With the annual publication "The Major Brands in Germany," we present successful company stories that follow the principle of Hartmut Esslinger: they have all deeply integrated design into their corporate strategy and are therefore able to offer a holistic customer experience via user-centered innovation and a consistently designed brand image.

Remaining successful requires anticipating the future.

Since the success of companies requires a high degree of adaptability, flexibility, and openness to innovation, we have grouped this issue under the triad "recreate. transform. be resilient." As different as the companies presented in this book are, they all have one thing in common: they have successfully positioned themselves as a strong brand and thus gained a decisive competitive advantage. A well-managed brand embodies consumers' expectations of the company and its products, makes it easier to find one's way around the market, and gives a sense of security and stability. I hope it can be seen that this always requires a willingness to transform. If you want to be successful and remain successful as a company, you have to anticipate the future. Tradition does not contradict this. Every transformation process takes place in the field of tension between revolution and evolution. The challenges that are emerging will force a profound transformation in all areas of our lives, not just for brands. Changing the way we live means changing almost everything; how we live, what we do, what we believe, and how we behave.

The circular economy will be one such transformational task that resilient companies will master as they prepare to reinvent themselves.

More than 350 well-known companies from various industries are already taking advantage of membership in our foundation and, in many cases, benefiting from the services offered by the German Design Council. We have formed a unique platform for collaborative dialogue — in the sense of the ability to think together — in order to use tensions between thoroughly opposing ideas and interests to find answers to difficult problems.

Design changes our behavior and actions.

In this way, we strengthen awareness of the importance of design in the spirit of the mission formulated by the German Parliament in 1953.
The importance of design is still too often misunderstood, underestimated. We live in a world designed by people. Almost everything that surrounds us has been designed. The things we design, the artificial, change our behavior and actions, and just as we have changed things through our designs, these things will then change us. They will affect how we behave and live. We design the world and the world, in turn, designs us. Therein lies the great responsibility of design and, at the same time, its power. In doing so, it will undoubtedly take the mobilization of many to change the way we live so that we can change the world for the better.

I am delighted that we have been constantly attracting new brands to walk this journey with us for 70 years. Be inspired by the brand success of the companies featured in this book. I look forward to the dialogue.

VITA
MIKE RICHTER

Mike Richter is the president of the German Design Council. He is also Dean of the Department of Design and Serial Entrepreneurship, Darmstadt University of Applied Sciences. He co-founded icon group, an international innovation catalyst; banbutsu, an experience facilitator platform; and Veritas Entertainment, an e-sports investor.

Why a resilient economy in the future is impossible to imagine without design and collaboration

ISABELLE VÉRILHAC
BEDA PRESIDENT – BUREAU OF EUROPEAN DESIGN ASSOCIATIONS

We are facing a major challenge, perhaps the largest that we have ever faced as a global society: climate change is an imminent consequence of the centuries we have spent innovating and the way we handled natural resources as a result, where almost all transformational developments are currently converging. Climate change, waves of migration, geopolitical battles for resources, and pandemics, for which industry and society are jointly responsible.

In this context, statistical projections of climate refugees and changes in biodiversity are juxtaposed with opportunities, which are reflected in the increase in business value developments in the area of sustainability (source: The New Climate Economy: The 2018 Report of the Global Commission on the Economy and Climate, which projected a 26 trillion dollar market in sustainability and a potential 65 million jobs by 2030).

This challenge, which can only be solved collaboratively, has reached Europe with the Green Deal and its associated climate goals for 2050. The New European Bauhaus (NEB) has defined this community task at the highest political level in Europe, and promotes interdisciplinary, cross-sector, and cross-industry teamwork by activating a framework for action. Beautiful, sustainable, together: this is how they would like to see the path toward a sustainable world in a new balance. But this motto is not the only indication that a major design task lies ahead in this project. The transformation also requires the structural power of design in particular, especially in the sense of its reflective, analytical, and problem-solving approach. As a process and a method, design takes on a decisive role in considering systemic dependencies and preventing their damaging consequences as much as possible.

With this understanding of design, BEDA has committed to being the first official partner of the New European Bauhaus Initiative as an umbrella organization of European design institutions and think tanks, and has supported the development of this incredible project, which involves citizens, experts, communities, and politicians. The participatory approach to the program corresponds to the method of design, which approaches the particular design task from the perspective of an individual. With the ability to think across disciplinary boundaries, designers have a crucial role to play in this great civilizational project during the collaborative process.

Designers possess a high degree of flexibility and adaptability, as they constantly evolve in order to anticipate the lifestyle of tomorrow, demonstrating their resilience and visionary spirit. BEDA (The Bureau of European Design Associations) supports talented individuals through the change and transformation of society, especially in the areas of digitalization and sustainability, to implement the Green Deal.

The Cultural and Creative Industries (CCIs) represented by BEDA describe, from the political promotional perspective, a broadly diversified and richly varied industry, which encompasses everything from architecture to literature to audiovisual medias, fashion, design, music, etc. It is one of the fourteen ecosystems defined by the European Industrial Strategy 2020 alongside the aerospace and defense industries, the transport and automobile industry, the healthcare sector and the tourist industry.

Still, the position of the CCIs should be perceived as a transverse sector rather than a vertical sector, as their reach and influence are critical to all ecosystems. Companies following best practice have integrated design deeply into their organization.

The function of the CCIs in further education (upskilling, reskilling) is extremely important for the changing job descriptions of tomorrow. In this context, BEDA has been involved as co-leader of the Pact for Skills due to its role as the link between its members and European politics, in order to take part in shaping the large-scale skills partnership for the Cultural and Creative Industries.

Our talents are a pool of creativity and sources of innovation, who produce sustainable economic success in all sectors. Designers and creatives are powerful engines for a new beginning for the entire industry.

European and national networks exist to facilitate connections and cooperation. Let's all master the current and future challenges together.

VITA
ISABELLE VÉRILHAC

Head of International Affairs and Innovation, Cité du design, Saint-Étienne, France, BEDA President. Focal point Saint-Étienne UNESCO City of Design

Isabelle Vérilhac holds a Post-Diploma in design & research, a Doctorate in material chemical physics, and gives lectures in industrial design. She was the director of the Saint-Étienne Medical Technologies Cluster from 2003 to 2007, and has worked in design, medical research and development activities.

For 12 years, she has been in charge of the relations with economic stakeholders at the Cité du design Saint-Étienne. She created and set up the materials resource center, the innovative uses and practices labs (LUPI®) and the Design Creative City Living Lab of the Cité du design. She coordinated the European Project IDeALL (Integrating Design for All in Living Labs), that combined design and user-centered Living Labs methodologies, and was one of the first design programs funded by the European Commission in 2012. She is in charge of the development and management of projects for economic, territorial, and societal projects. Since the beginning of 2019, Isabelle has been the International Manager and Coordinator of Saint-Étienne UNESCO City of Design and, as a member for some years of the Board of The Bureau of European Design Associations (BEDA), she was elected President in May 2021.

Enduring, adaptable, crisis-proof

LUTZ DIETZOLD
CEO GERMAN DESIGN COUNCIL

Suddenly, it appears — crises usually come as a surprise, and the next one probably will as well. But what possibilities exist to prepare ahead of time, as a company and as an industry? In our opinion, there is a clear connection between constant flexibility and the ability to survive turbulent times. This leads to several interesting questions: How are design and resilience connected? Can good design improve the stability and adaptability of products, businesses, or even entire industries? Questions that are highly valuable, particularly in difficult times.

As the German Design Council, we have supported the German economy for almost 70 years, and not a few of our members have existed for just as long or even longer. They were seven decades that also contained difficult times to overcome — but we still have the same companies on our side and have asked ourselves, what kind of an influence does good design have on long-term success? Are strong brands and companies with high design standards more resilient? From the perspective of the German Design Council, the answer is a clear, "yes!" Companies with a deeply rooted design strategy are more resistant to crises. This can also be well substantiated with regard to the different areas of design. Sophisticated design can work in different contexts and environments. We can begin our observations at the product level: well-designed products can still fit into the most diverse environments over a long period of time. Proven classics in furniture or consumer goods cater to diverse functions and aesthetic requirements. They achieve a high-level of adaptability specifically because of their durability. The products' expandability or repair capacity are also important features of resilience: if one component should fail, it can be replaced or repaired quickly without making the entire product useless. Product families and systems that are able to be consistently updated and expanded, without having to be completely replaced, obtain a similar effect. At that point, there is a certain level of complexity that has been reached where good design management is necessary to maintain a balance between consistency and innovation. An additional advantage that increases the customer's trust and creates a stronger bond with the brand.

Good brand communication builds on content, is honest and authentic, and can therefore also make necessary changes in course much more credibly than with laboriously constructed stories that are difficult to adapt when the general conditions change.

Further important factors related to resilience are economic stability and the ability to act. Brands with high design standards do not market their products primarily on the basis of price and are therefore not as exposed to the risk of falling into a spiral of pricing pressure in times of crisis, which can quickly lead to economic distress.

The term resilience is often used more broadly to include improving conditions as a new standard. That is where the connection is made to continual learning, developing, and innovating capabilities, which are inherent in sophisticated design. The ability to renew, for which our member companies are exemplary, is a glowing example of the adaptability of a company. Let's take Bosch, a family-owned company that has remained compelling through technological advances and good design consistently throughout its more than 130-year history. Or the company Dräger, also more than 130 years old, which has continuously dealt with difficult situations as a specialist in medical technology and safety engineering in its products, and has obviously been good at transferring the insights gained from this to corporate management and design. Or Festo, which has been successful again and again in using pneumatics to create the most unbelievable things, most recently the motor inside Cobots, cooperative robots, which work together with people. The Deutsche Telekom as well, as an independent company that was only founded in 1995, shows how a company in the dynamic field of technology infrastructure can continually evolve and adapt. Just as impressive as the exemplary large companies mentioned are the many medium-sized companies among our members, which are also represented in this book. They all use good design as a factor in a resilient company that can continue to create innovative and compelling solutions to major challenges.

VITA
LUTZ DIETZOLD

Lutz Dietzold (born in 1966) has been Chief Executive Officer of the German Design Council since 2002. He has been a member of the German Design Museum Foundation since 2011, as well as a member of the advisory council of the German Federal Ecodesign Award, the Mia Seeger Foundation, and numerous other panels and juries.

Dietzold regularly publishes articles and holds international lectures on topics related to design, brands, and innovation.

Strong brands and the stories behind them.

MENTOR

INTEGRATED LED LIGHT
SOLUTIONS AND HMI
COMPONENTS

With a major passion for the subject of light,
MENTOR-Group from Erkrath creates custom solutions that enable their customers to break new
ground in terms of product development and design.

Credit: Werbepartner Huth GmbH

As providers of integrated light solutions, MENTOR executes LED based lighting components at the highest technical level. The customers of the North Rhein Westphalian company come from the automotive industry in particular, as well as other areas with design relevant products. Their specialized light solutions are created in close cooperation with the client: everything, from the technical concept to the development, visualization and tool construction, up to the manufacturing of the finished components, is delivered from the same provider. Since demand is steadily increasing and requirements can be very different depending on the project, Mentor employs a wide-ranging technology portfolio in the area of fiber optics. This enables the manufacturer to respond flexibly to individual customer requirements and create customized solutions.

The components that MENTOR produces are not subject to typical design criteria. The actual company product is good lighting and its effects. Designers use it as a multi-faceted design tool that offers practically limitless options for product and industrial design. High quality light can be integrated into a wide variety of products and offers added functional value. Through the way that MENTOR manufactures specialized lighting components, novel products can be developed that are contemporary, aesthetically pleasing, and robust. Light provides for more security, comfort, and orientation, among other things, and can serve as a component of communication or an information item.

MENTOR was founded in 1920 by the engineer Dr. Paul Mozar in Düsseldorf as a factory for electrical engineering and precision mechanics and registered as a trademark. Since then, the brand name has stood for the strength of the family-owned company, which offers excellent counsel to its clients. In 1965 Dr. Ehrhard Weyer took over the company and built it up into one of the leading German manufacturers for electronic components. In 1996, the product range was expanded into the field of optoelectronics by light guide systems. Since 2003, the Managing Partner and CEO Wido Weyer has led the company — and has done so since 2021 with his son, Dennis Weyer, serving as Managing Partner and CVO. Today, MENTOR is among the world's largest suppliers with its light guide range. Its core competence in the field of LED light was specifically expanded by the founding of the MENTOR-Light Group in 2009.

The company uses its extensive software and hardware equipment to solve demanding lighting tasks. The virtual light development and its visualization happens in the in-house light laboratory. The specialized LED light solutions are used by customers from the fields of automation, electronics, communication technology, building technology and medical technology, as well as plant and machine construction. Roughly 80 percent of the product offering consists of components specifically developed for the customer. The spectrum of technology that is used in-house by MENTOR is large and ranges from plastic injection molding to electronic and light development to tool construction. Through close cooperation between the different departments, individual lighting solutions are created that are perfectly tailored to the project.

FACTS AND FIGURES

PRODUCTS
integrated LED light solutions and HMI components

LOCATIONS
Erkrath, further locations in Germany, Poland, Tunisia and China

FOUNDER
Ing. Dr. Paul Mozar
(1920, Düsseldorf)

OWNER
the third generation of the Weyer Family

EMPLOYEES
260 in Germany

SALES
worldwide

WEBSITE
mentor.de

Unique and captivating lighting solutions are created at Mentor using decades of knowledge, a major passion for the subject of light, and the most modern technology.

Credit: Werbepartner Huth GmbH

Credit: Studio Salewski GmbH

Busch-Jaeger Elektro GmbH

ELECTRICAL TECHNOLOGY

Custom designing the home, both functionally and aesthetically:
that is Busch-Jaeger. For more than 140 years the successful
company has centered its focus on people and their individual
requirements.

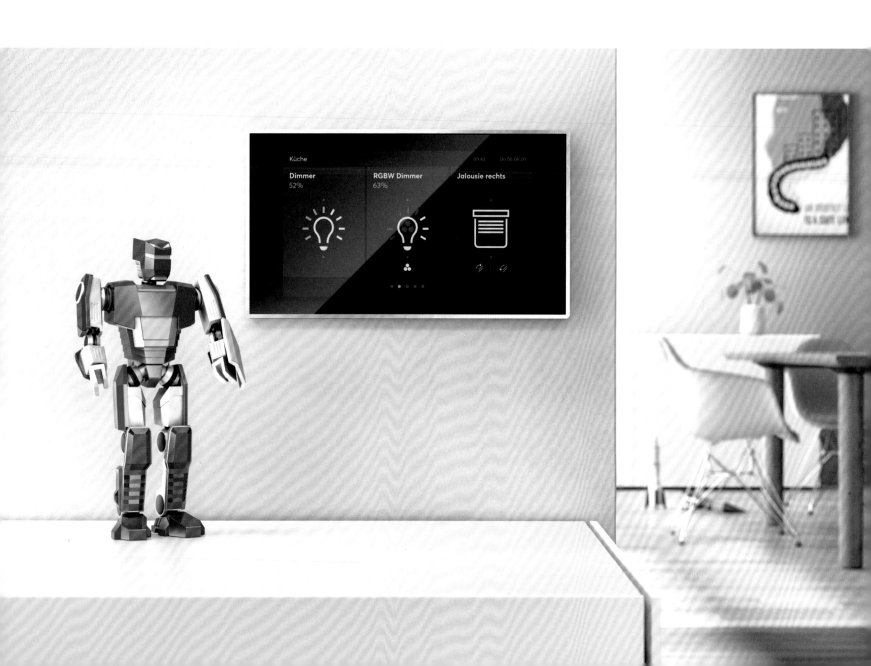

The market leader for electrical installation technology in Germany, Austria and the Netherlands offers flexible smarter home solutions, which are solidly aligned with the specific needs of their users and are not only persuasive in their function, but also offer added value for the modern home with a view to their design.

The spectrum of approximately 6,000 products and solutions from Busch-Jaeger Elektro GmbH ranges from well-designed switch ranges to innovative network systems for building systems technology in smart homes and smart buildings.

The chronicle of Busch-Jaeger Elektro GmbH stands out due to numerous pioneering achievements and innovative products in the electrical installation technology sector. What Heinrich Jaeger started with, the founding of his metal turning factory, is today a market leading company in electrical installation technology with two locations in Germany. Busch-Jaeger Elektro GmbH, which has belonged to BBC (now ABB) since 1969, employs 1,300 people in its two domestic plants in Lüdenscheid and Aue alone. They export to more than 60 countries around the globe and there are licensing and production cooperations with partner companies in Spain, Czech Republic, Finland, and Asia.

The constant evolution of the brand, a detailed observation of their target groups and their needs, as well as a unique combination of tradition and innovation are the ingredients of Busch-Jaeger's success. The current, individual needs of the customer are considered equally as much as possible future requirements.

With the #smartertogether campaign, Busch-Jaeger has been focusing on the aspects of trust and quality, consciousness and perspective, as well as comfort and lifestyle. The individual desire to have security, sustainability, and fun at home is their main focus and creates the foundation of the brand.

The design of Busch-Jaeger products and solutions is captivating in its precision and simplicity, is easy to operate due to reducing down to the essentials, and uses durable, long-lasting materials as well as high-quality workmanship. The desires and needs of the client remain at the center of the focus. They rely on constant research and development in order to remain innovative.

The design motto of Busch-Jaeger is to impress with clarity and functionality. Numerous national and international awards have proven that this succeeds in the best possible way. They confirm the company's design and quality standards and motivate it to maintain its strength in innovation and remain open to change, exciting topics, and interesting perspectives. In eventful times, you want to create new things and preserve the tried and true. That is what the strong brand Busch-Jaeger stands for.

FACTS AND FIGURES

PRODUCTS
electrical installation materials

LOCATIONS
Lüdenscheid and Aue, partner companies in Spain, Czech Republic, Finland, and Asia

FOUNDERS
Hans-Curt Jaeger together with his brother Georg
(1879, Lüdenscheid)

OWNER
concern and 100 percent subsidiary of ABB;
Chairman of the Board:
Adalbert Neumann

EMPLOYEES
approx. 1,200 in Germany (2021)

SALES
worldwide via architects, designers, electricians, wholesale

WEBSITE
busch-jaeger.de

BUSCH-JAEGER

Busch-Jaeger stands for electrical installation technology that makes life easier and future-proof. As market leader we think in generations and take on responsibility by creating a sustainable future.

Geck®

FIXTURES AND FITTINGS, SHOPPING TROLLEYS, PRICING DISPLAYS, AND DIGITAL SOLUTIONS FOR RETAILERS AND LOGISTICS.

A small product with a large effect: the Geck Hook revolutionized the point of sale in the 1960s. Today, Geck® also offers the most modern digital solutions.

Strategically optimized and perfectly crafted: displays from Geck®.

At home in every store: Geck® shopping trolleys.

A smart idea becomes a timeless classic: the patented Geck Hook can find a use everywhere in brick-and-mortar stores. Nearly everyone who goes shopping has seen one at one time. It is used as a functional display fitting with one or two hooks and can be easily installed in metal peg panels used in displays, as well as all conventional back panel systems. Through innovative developments from the House of Geck®, displays that have already been stocked with goods can also be regrouped effortlessly. While the Geck Hook presents products on offer at the point of sale in an optimal way, it also remains modestly in the background. These practical display fittings made from galvanized metal have already been manufactured more than 300 million times and are the world market leader in their segment.

The success story of this fifth generation, family-owned business began in 1852, when Johann Diedrich Geck established his company in Westphalian Mühlenrahmede, a neighborhood of Altena. After completing an apprenticeship as a blacksmith, he moved on to creating chains and other metal supplies for the agriculture industry. His successors did the same. As a result, Geck® was already able to look back on a history that was more than 100 years old when they revolutionized the concept of self-service in the retail sector with their clever hook system.

Starting in the 1950s, the innovative company gradually changed its product range from wire goods and furniture fittings to retail accessories and display fittings such as the Geck Hook. With the success of discounters, shopping centers and larger specialty stores, in the following decades Geck® developed into a leading international manufacturer of customized, integrated solutions for the point of sale. Three hundred fifty people are currently employed at the Altena, Lüdenscheid, and Luckau locations.

Today, this progressive company also offers its customers digital solutions, in addition to display fittings, displays and shopping trolleys- because for this manufacturer, traditionally involved in metalworking, digital transformation means much more than just the digitalization of their own processes in development, production, logistics and administration. As a competent partner to brick-and-mortar stores, Geck® began an evolutionary development of intelligent technologies for the point of sale five years ago, in order to make the insights that online retailers gain from their analysis options possible for the physical store and create a cross-channel customer journey.

It was a long way to go from chains for agriculture to the developing of digital solutions. Geck® was created from the courage of its founder; the creative power of its employees has turned it into a world market leader. Innovation will continue to be the driver of this company in the future.

FACTS AND FIGURES

PRODUCTS
fixtures and fittings, shopping trolleys, pricing displays, and digital solutions for retail stores, administration, logistics, etc.

LOCATIONS
Altena, Lüdenscheid, Luckau

FOUNDER
Johann Diedrich Geck
(1852, Altena)

OWNERS
the 5th generation of the Geck family

EMPLOYEES
350 (2022)

SALES
Germany and Europe

WEBSITE
geck.de

RZB Lighting

ELECTRICAL INDUSTRY

WE MAKE LIGHT.

What began with the production of electrical supplies and porcelain luminaires became an international success story. The family-owned company RZB Rudolf Zimmermann, Bamberg GmbH, founded by Rudolf Zimmermann in 1939, today belongs to one of the most influential companies in the international lighting industry. For RZB, "Made in Germany" means, "Made in Bamberg."

The extensive product portfolio covers nearly every lighting requirement: interior and exterior lighting, security lighting, light management systems, UV-C air sterilization systems. RZB offers not only a comprehensive range of lighting systems, but also guides and supports their clients from the first step to the last: while planning the lighting, during the system programming, the commissioning process, monitoring, and much more. "Thinking of light holistically," is the motto they live by and which sets the company apart from its competitors. Direct customer contact and comprehensive service play an important role in that.

The company is distinctive with its holistic view of technical product features, energy efficiency, and design. The expectation of getting as close to perfection as possible has paid off. In 2021, RZB received the TOP 100 award for the fourth time, confirming that it is one of the most innovative companies in the German SME sector. RZB has already won more than 75 internationally recognized design awards for their design work, including Red Dot, GDA, and iF.

With the LINEDO system, RZB has created a veritable revolution in LED trunking systems. In LINEDO, the mounting channel and continuous-line luminaire form a single unit, making installation significantly easier. The benefits and areas of application, on the other hand, are maximized. Superior technology makes the system outstandingly efficient, future-proof, and flexible in use. The stylish, minimalistic single-component continuous line luminaire system can be configured via web and app, cuts installation time in half, and is deployable almost everywhere, from industrial buildings and supermarkets to architecturally demanding environments such as museums or even sacred buildings.

Future sustainability: for the company, this includes continuous testing and improvement of all products as well as the development of new product innovations with added value for customers and the environment. Resilient: that means taking responsibility for the Bamberg location and its employees in addition to securing high quality standards. Globalization, current world events and the issue of sustainability also continue to present RZB with new challenges. The challenges are being met by opening up new areas of business. Digitalization has been especially accelerated over the last few years. The online presence has been developed and expanded to include, among other things, 3D animated visuals, product videos, and interactive digital brochures- a plus for the environment and the customer.

RZB has been honored with the bronze medal from EcoVadis for their sustainability activities. With the courage to continually improve, the company feels that it is well equipped for the future, in order to play a decisive role in the further development of light.

FACTS AND FIGURES

PRODUCTS
interior lighting, exterior lighting, security lighting, light management systems, UV-C air sterilization systems, consulting, planning, commissioning, related services

LOCATIONS
Subsidiaries in Austria, Switzerland, Northern Europe, France, Asia-Pacific, and the United Arab Emirates.

FOUNDER
Rudolf Zimmermann
(1939, Bamberg)

OWNER
sole shareholder Dr. Alexander Zimmermann

EMPLOYEES
more than 700 (2022)

SALES
nearly worldwide; B2B in the DACH region and Europe, in addition to sales partners in over 70 countries and trade partners in Dubai and Malaysia

WEBSITE
rzb.de

Strong light for strong brands. With 360° light competence, RZB is the partner with a comprehensive and far-reaching vision. Photo source: Linus Lintner Fotografie | Berlin

Tojo – flexible elegance and functionality

FURNITURE MANUFACTURING

Timeless, simple design distinguishes the furniture produced by Tojo.
Since its founding by Gerald Schatz in June of 2000, the products
made by Tojo Möbel GmbH in Schorndorf are characterized by their
elegance, functionality, ecology, and economy.

The special feature of Tojo furniture lies in its flexibility. The first products were beds where the size could be changed. The bed model Tojo-vario, for example, expands like an accordion and can accompany you from childhood into adulthood, or offer space to one or more guests. The organic bed is created completely without screws, fittings, paint, and varnish.

The company works together with various designers. They place a high value on sustainability: all the wood, without exception, comes from sustainable forestry and is not treated with wood preservative. The beds in particular are made of untreated wood; for other products, untreated, FSC-certified medium density fiberboard (MDF) is used, which is coated in a white or anthracite color melamine resin. Because of this, the simple Tojo furniture is able to fit perfectly into any home or office in terms of color.

The production facilities in Germany, Northern Italy, and Hungary work with minimal waste. All the furniture is completely recyclable, with the exception of the screws and fittings, and is packaged disassembled, which allows for a more economical transport. In addition to their own online shop, the company markets its products via designer furniture stores in particular: primarily in Germany, but also in numerous European countries as well as in Japan, Australia, and South Korea.

The range of products has been significantly expanded over the years. At the moment, Tojo offers a wide range of seating, small furniture pieces, and children's furniture in addition to beds, racks, and closets and remains current with clever ideas, simple elegance, and affordable functional design.

In times of increasing raw material costs and shortages, a major strength of Tojo Furniture lies in their core feature of expandability and sustainability. In the areas of closets and shelving, there are no limits to how far the furniture can be expanded thanks to its high level of flexibility and comprehensive functions which are sure to impress. Therefore, whoever chooses a piece of Tojo furniture can use it in many different ways and enlarge it, scale it down, or change its function and location.

Tojo Furniture has been honored with numerous design awards. Just two years after its founding, the second bed in the collection (called Tojo-vario) won the International Design Award from the Design Center Stuttgart. Today, a variety of furniture pieces have won many awards, among them the Interior Innovation Award and the German Design Award. The brand Tojo has also been distinguished with the German Brand Award, among others.

In 2016, Tojo was accepted to the German Design Council. A further milestone was reached in 2022, when the company moved into their new building in Schorndorf with their eight current employees.

FACTS AND FIGURES

PRODUCTS
wooden furniture

LOCATION
Schorndorf

FOUNDER
Gerald Schatz
(2000, Schorndorf)

OWNER
Gerald Schatz

EMPLOYEES
8 (2022)

SALES
Europe, Japan, Australia, and South Korea, via designer furniture stores and the online shop

WEBSITE
tojo.de

The brand Telekom: on its way to becoming the "Leading Digital Telco"

TELECOMMUNICATIONS

The Deutsche Telekom has evolved into one of the leading global players in the branch of telecommunications. As the most valuable digital telecommunications company in Europe and the second most valuable worldwide, the company has been on course for the future for years. In pursuit of its latest goal, "Leading Digital Telco," the concern has aligned its presence step by step with its new brand strategy, in order to offer its customers a uniform brand experience worldwide. The experience is primarily focused on people's participation in digital life, sustainable actions, and social cohesion.

One company. One brand. One goal. Telekom would like to unite all national subsidiaries worldwide under one strong global brand and an iconic brand identity. This consolidated presence is the foundation for further growth and a uniform perception in all markets. Using a transnational brand architecture, they offer their customers a clear orientation and support efficient and effective brand and communication management.

"Our global branding approach is a significant support to our international digital and sustainable business strategy," explained Ulrich Klenke, Chief Brand Officer of Deutsche Telekom. "A purpose, a brand architecture, a logo, a slogan, and a brand design: we want to make the Telekom brand an experience for all people worldwide."

Stronger. Simpler. More modern.
Telekom doesn't only have a clear focus on its brand strategy. At the beginning of 2022, they significantly changed their logo and optimized it for use at digital touchpoints. The well-known "T" took on a new role and will become an even greater focus of communication in the future. No longer acting as a mere sender identifier, the iconic T will now be staged according to the particular occasion and target group. The logo is a strong symbol for the digital optimism that is a hallmark of the brand. As a "lighthouse," it symbolizes the quality and strength of the Telekom network as well as the expertise in innovative digital technologies that enable society to overcome current and future challenges together. This is always done with the goal of enriching people's lives and making it possible for every individual to participate digitally.

In addition to the logo, the company color, magenta, is and will remain a central distinguishing feature. Few companies in the world are so clearly recognized and remembered by their brand color. In addition to the recognition of the color, the word "magenta" also has a role to play: in the future, the term will be used in the transnational structuring of the product portfolio and guarantees a clear differentiation from the competition. In combination with the Liquid Brand Design system, introduced in 2020, the logo and color are the foundation for consolidating Telekom's perception as a global brand.

A brand with international charisma.

One of the most well-known and valuable brands in the world.
Today, Deutsche Telekom is one of the most well-known and valuable brands worldwide and by far the most valuable telecommunications brand in Europe. Various ratings and indices list the company among the top 20 brands worldwide and confirm its positive business development and successful brand strategy.

A brand that is on the way to becoming the Leading Digital Telco.

The T is at the center of communication and can be staged according to the particular subject and target group.

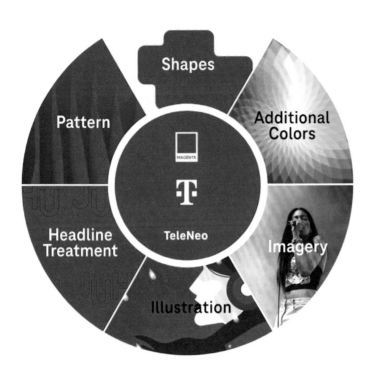

FACTS AND FIGURES

INDUSTRY
With approximately 250 million mobile customers, 26 million fixed-network lines, and 21 million broadband lines, Deutsche Telekom is one of the world's leading integrated telecommunications companies.

PRODUCTS
Products and services related to fixed-network lines, broadband lines, mobile communications, the internet and internet-based TV; ICT solutions in the B2B field

LOCATIONS
In more than 50 countries worldwide, headquarters in Bonn, North Rhein Westphalia

EMPLOYEES
216,528 employees worldwide

ANNUAL TURNOVER
108.8 billion € (2021)

WEBSITE
telekom.de

Above: The Liquid Brand Design essentially consists of fixed elements that ensure recognizability. The outside ring contains flexible design elements for creative storytelling. Below: The company color, magenta, remains a central distinguishing feature. As a carrier surface for communication, it can take on an appropriate form depending on the context and contact point.

Bethmann Bank

FINANCIAL SERVICES

Can a bank be one of the oldest private banks in Germany while simultaneously one of the most modern? That is not a contradiction for Bethmann Bank. Whether analog, digital, or with new technologies in the future: change has always been part of their everyday business.

GENUINE.
SUSTAINABLE.
PRIVATE.

heir values remain the same: the people, their customers as well as their employees, are at the center in order to shape society for the benefit of everyone.

Founded in 1712, today Bethmann Bank is one of the top three providers of private banking in Germany and primarily supports private clients, institutional clients and businesses. They belong to the Dutch ABN AMRO, one of the strongest banks financially in Europe. With 14 locations, they are represented in every important economic area in Germany and are also well-connected internationally.

As one of the few private banks that offer individual consultations, their focus is not on their own products, but on clear, understandable and sustainable solutions for their clients. At the heart of the business is asset management: over 80 percent of newly invested client funds now go into this sustainable service. For example, since the beginning of 2022 they have offered the "Entrepreneur & Enterprise" service: a team of specialized corporate bankers examine private assets as well as company assets alongside private client advisors. The service is especially relevant for family-run businesses who are unable to separate one from the other.

History and modernity united.

Sustainable investing and social action are inseparable at Bethmann Bank. Sustainability is not only a catchphrase: the asset management department has offered sustainable funds since 2011 and an external, independent Sustainability Advisory Board has been in place for just as long. Since 2021, clients have received a report with an overview of how much CO_2 a sustainable securities account saves in contrast to a conventional securities account. Banking operations have changed as well: the bank has used green energy since 2013, its car and travel policies have been reformed, the bank's headquarters in Frankfurt have moved from the main office "Bethmannhof" into a LEED certified building, and they are working on becoming CO_2 neutral.

Change has been a constant companion for more than three centuries. Clients of the bank include Kaiser Friedrich the Great and the family of Johann Wolfgang von Goethe. Bethmann was involved in the financing of the Eiffel Tower and in the founding of young companies such as Siemens and Krupp. Nevertheless, they have never rested on their laurels. The bank has constantly adapted to new conditions, still to this day focusing on the ever-changing needs of their customers. In some areas, Bethmann has even been a pioneer. They have offered sustainable investments since 2011, and invested considerably in IT even in the years before the pandemic, through which the contact with their clients has been, and remains, seamlessly managed digitally — an important foundation for a successful future.

FACTS AND FIGURES

PRODUCTS
Asset management, investment advisory, Entrepreneur & Enterprise, private equity, philanthropy, inheritance planning, lending, wholesale

LOCATIONS
Frankfurt am Main (headquarters) as well as 13 more German cities; ABN AMRO: 13 countries worldwide

FOUNDERS
Splitgerber and Daum (1712), Berlin

OWNER
ABN AMRO

EMPLOYEES
550 in Germany (2021); about 20,000 worldwide in the parent company ABN AMRO

SALES
Germany

WEBSITE
bethmannbank.de

Mauser

CONSTRUCTION AND
MANUFACTURING OF STEEL
FURNISHING SYSTEMS

High-quality steel furniture from Mauser Furnishing Systems is functional, sustainable, and long-lasting. The company from Korbach constructs its systems with a passion for the steel material.

Tried and tested millions of times by commercial end-users; the universal double door cabinet made by Mauser has been manufactured and sold for more than 60 years. A variety of models, sizes, features, and colors ensure that it can meet any requirements. In the 1980s/1990s, the "Mauser Cabinet" for storing filing cards could have been found in just about any doctor's office. Beyond that, Mauser steel cabinets have served as durable storage space in offices, schools, factories, and archives for a long time.

The company was founded in 1896 by Alfons Mauser in Oberndorf am Neckar, in Baden-Württemberg, as a factory for sheet steel products and steel mesh. 1921 saw the purchase of factory facilities in Waldeck in North Hessen, and the founding of the Mauser-Werke GmbH, which was later taken over by his son who expanded their product range. The production of steel furniture began in 1929. Starting in 1953, tables, seating, office furniture and steel cabinets for warehouses and factories were built in Korbach, in Hessen, their headquarters today. Today, Dr. Martin Sagel runs the company. With the guiding principle, "Just do it sustainably," Mauser makes their company philosophy clear, which is linked to a voluntary commitment to action for a sustainable future.

The Mauser storage furniture is produced from sustainable steel, in contrast to many competitor products. That has a decisive advantage: the steel material is extremely robust, unaffected by either fire or water. Thanks to the high load-bearing capacity of the material, Mauser cabinets are also able to be transported while they are filled. And after the working life of a piece of steel furniture is over, the material is able to be 100% recycled — again and again.

Manufactured steel offers a sustainable, resource-saving basis for the production of new steel products. Mauser uses steel sheets in the production of their furniture, while galvanized sheets are built into their shelving systems. Thanks to its special manufacturing and materials expertise, the company can shape the material into a wide variety of configurations.

The design line, "element.x," is a stylishly designed storage system for the furnishing of offices and living spaces. Its highly durable, double walled steel modules can be combined into cabinets, counters, display cases, shelves, room partitions, and lowboards. They can be designed in one- or two-tone RAL colors. The distinguishing feature of the system is the chrome-plated corner connectors made from die cast zinc, which serve as mitre joints. Stacking four modules creates a distinctive "x."

The new partition and acoustic systems from Mauser have proven to be especially flexible. The individual elements from the series, "conexius.w" can be assembled into new types of furniture over and over as needed. So, an acoustic wall can become a shelving unit or a wall of planter boxes that also serve as a room partition. For furniture systems such as these, and for 125 years of development, construction, and production of high-quality innovations, the company was recognized as, "Brand of the Century 2022," in the product category steel furniture.

FACTS AND FIGURES

PRODUCTS
furniture systems made of steel

LOCATION
Korbach, Hessen

FOUNDER
Dr.-Ing. e. h. Alfons Mauser
(1896, Oberndorf am Neckar)

OWNER
Vauth-Sagel Holding (since 2004)

EMPLOYEES
250 (2022)

SALES
Europe via specialty stores and mail order

WEBSITE
mauser.com

mauser
Ideen aus Stahl – seit 1896

Steel creates architecture, element.x is as compelling in the home office as in the open-plan office; Multi-story system of mobile shelving RR409 in archives.

MARTOR

TOOLS, PPE

Professional tools primarily fulfill a precise, predetermined function. The award-winning MARTOR design has influenced functionality, safety, and individually perceived value equally.

The handle of a knife is just part of the daily work routine for workers in industry and trade. Whether it's a fast cut through tape or a precise cut through material: a sharp knife makes the professional's work considerably easier. Additionally, the ergonomic design is decisively responsible for the handling of the knife. Ergonomics help with work efficiency on one side and prevent work accidents on the other.

Over more than 80 years, MARTOR has evolved as a third generation, family-run business into an international quality and technology leader for safe and efficient cutting. In doing so, MARTOR has used its reliable instinct for the needs of the user and its strong technological knowledge in order to develop and produce innovative and long-lasting quality products over and over. The results are product and design classics, including the internationally successful, first TÜV certified safety knife in the world, called PROFI, equipped with an automatic blade retractor. And, the first safety knife in the world with a fully automatic blade retractor, one safety level higher. Their latest coup: with the squeeze-grip knives SECUPRO 625, SECUPRO MARTEGO, and SECUPRO MERAK, the Nürnberg Institute for Health and Ergonomics has certified three work knives as, "ergonomic products," for the first time.

With functionality, design, and quality, MARTOR has been successful in developing benchmark products in the three most common safety knife categories (concealed blades, fully automatic blade retraction, automatic blade retraction). The company relies equally on modern production methods as well as a high degree of expert craftsmanship — during the obligatory manual quality check, for example.

The brand-typical MARTOR design has garnered the company numerous awards, among others the Red Dot Design Award, the German Design Award, the pro-K Award and the iF Design Award.

MARTOR does not only aim to please the eye of its beholder with its product design. Design elements such as clear lines, cyan colored operating elements, and the label on the product support the user in the intuitive and therefore particularly safe and efficient handling of the product.

In any case, MARTOR attaches great importance to the fact that not only its cutting tools, but also its services are consistently conceived of and designed with the customer in mind. The same goes for its appearance as an accessible, modern, and friendly company. Their new logo, "THE SAFER WAY TO CUT," is both a requirement and a mission. Everyone that has anything to do with professional cutting can be sure that they have found the optimal solution with MARTOR.

FACTS AND FIGURES

PRODUCTS
safety knives; products and services related to safe cutting

LOCATIONS
Solingen (central office), USA and France; partners and retailers worldwide

FOUNDER
E. Helmut Beermann (1940, Solingen)

OWNER
Sonja Hendricks (sole shareholder)

EMPLOYEES
150/30 (domestically/internationally)

SALES
distribution in more than 80 countries internationally, with a focus on the PPE and tools trade

WEBSITE
martor.com

martor

THE SAFER WAY TO CUT.

CUTTING-EDGE CONVENIENCE: the brand's idea is manifested in products, services, and premises and can be experienced by customers and employees at all times.

RTL

MEDIA AND ENTERTAINMENT

RTL has evolved from a broadcaster to Europe's leading entertainment brand. The brand stands for an entire spectrum of entertainment – from good entertainment to unbiased journalism, from TV to streaming, from content to tech, from design to data.

FACTS AND FIGURES

PRODUCTS
media and entertainment,
Platform RTL+

LOCATIONS
Cologne, Hamburg, Berlin,
15 further cities

FOUNDERS
CLT and Bertelsmann/UFA

OWNER
RTL Group

EMPLOYEES
7,500 (2022)

SALES
Germany,
online worldwide

WEBSITE
rtl.de

The story of RTL began on a rooftop in Luxembourg. Two brothers with pioneering spirits, Marcel and François Anen, founded the Association Radio Luxembourg in 1925. For a long time, no one could have imagined that the small radio station would one day develop into one of the largest European entertainment networks. In 1957, "Radio Luxembourg" began to broadcast in Germany for a few hours per day. On July 15, broadcaster Pierre Nilles uttered his first announcement in German. "Beginning today," he said, "we will broadcast a program with light music daily from 2pm to 4pm. Please get in touch if you happen to hear us."

At that point in time, no one could have guessed how much one of the first European commercial broadcasters would change the media landscape in Germany. Currently, RTL Germany has its headquarters in Cologne and offices in 17 additional locations; the most important ones are in Hamburg and Berlin. The company describes its expertise as being in, "content, tech, and data for good entertainment and unbiased journalism."

As the leading entertainment brand across all media genres, RTL Germany employs approximately 7,500 people with an annual turnover of 2.43 million euros (2021). The cross-media brand portfolio has been designed to "reach every person in Germany." Additionally, the platform "RTL+" is being expanded into an all-encompassing media offering. In the future, subscribers will be able to view not only films and series', shows, documentaries, sports and information, but also an extensive offering of music, exclusive podcasts, an audiobook library as well as access to premium digital magazines. Their motto is, "see more, hear more, read more." The new corporate company design reflects this attitude and signals that, "RTL is colorful," because the logo doesn't contain only one color, but an entire spectrum of colors.

International crises and a more aggressive political climate have changed society. It is of even more importance as a media company to maintain a clear position and take on more responsibility. RTL Germany wants to set an example, company spokespeople say. "We are committed to diversity, solidarity, sustainability, and humanity. We speak plainly, straightforwardly, and at eye level. We inspire people to see things differently, to tackle challenges or to make better decisions, large or small." The company wants to meet this expectation with positive entertainment and unbiased journalism, and not only in Germany. RTL is to be developed into the leading European entertainment brand.

Whoever wants to be successful and remain successful must anticipate the future.

PROF. MIKE RICHTER

SCHRAMM
Workshops

FURNITURE INDUSTRY/
MATTRESS MANUFACTURING

As an internationally successful premium brand, the bed manufacturer SCHRAMM connects traditional craftsmanship with a high level of innovation and works beyond the usual mass production.

For three generations, the brand SCHRAMM has stood for quality and the highest level of sleep comfort, which has been consistently further developed. The family-owned company was founded in 1923 by Karl Schramm in Enkenbach-Alsenborn as an upholstery and saddlery business. In the mid 1960s, the company began to specialize in the manufacturing of high-quality mattresses and base mattresses. This was followed by the development of their own bed creations as well as fully integrated two mattress systems. Today, the internationally successful SCHRAMM workshops are located in Winnweiler, in Rhineland Pfalz. The company's portfolio contains patented sleep systems and exclusively designed beds, some of which are created by working with well-known designers.

SCHRAMM stands for long-lasting values and sustainable quality. With their extensive knowledge, from traditional craftsmanship to modern production organization, the roughly 190 employees of SCHRAMM workshops create first class sleeping comfort. The production of SCHRAMM beds is characterized by a high level of precision and personal dedication. Every bed is handmade to order in their modern factory and is therefore truly unique. The right mix of precious materials and an experienced team with good intuition makes the extraordinary quality possible. With their innovative products, "handmade in Germany," SCHRAMM represents an opposing position to the usual mass production of today and is a leader in the market. The brand's mindset and approach include the fact that SCHRAMM will remain a family-owned company that produces in Germany in the future.

The highly specialized SCHRAMM team develops innovative products and systems for good and refreshing sleep. In the brand's manufactured mattresses, permanently elastic springs are used that are manufactured according to internationally unique methods and are resistant to fatigue and overloading. In order to achieve a high level of sleep comfort, SCHRAMM also adds varied spring forces, called formulas, which adapt individually to the lying body. With the well-known comfort of the beds, reasonable use of natural materials, and sustainable craftsmanship, SCHRAMM has made a name for itself internationally. Perfectly-formed, unique pieces of sleep culture are created in the workshops through the know-how of the team.

The company's vision includes numerous facets: SCHRAMM has focused on private customers with the product lines PUREBEDS, ORIGINS, and ORIGINS COMPLETE, as well as GRAND CRU. The SAVOY line makes a high level of sleep comfort possible in the hospitality industry. The beds in this line are not only successful in the domestic as well as international market, but have also been recognized with numerous prestigious design awards, include the award, "Brand of the Century," awarded by the Zeit-Verlagsgruppe.

Proven traditions can pave the way into the future and the SCHRAMM workshops succeed in this in an exemplary fashion. The tradition-rich family-owned company will celebrate its 100 year anniversary in the year 2023.

FACTS AND FIGURES

PRODUCTS
bed systems, mattresses, and occasional furniture in the premium segment

LOCATION
Winnweiler, Rheinland-Pfalz

FOUNDER
Karl Schramm
(1923, Enkenbach-Alsenborn)

MANAGING DIRECTOR
Martin Kaus

EMPLOYEES
190

SALES
B2B trade partners; DACH region, BENELUX countries, France, Italy, Spain, Denmark, Liechtenstein, Czech Republic, Lithuania, Ukraine, Latvia, Asia

WEBSITE
schramm-werkstaetten.com

SCHRAMM
home of sleep

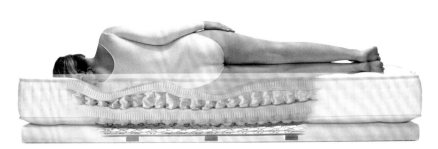

55

OutNature by PreZero

PAPER AND PULP INDUSTRY

With more than 23 million tons of annual production volume, paper, cardboard, and paperboard are among some of the most important materials. OutNature presents a versatile, innovative, and sustainable fiber alternative.

GROUNDED IN THE FUTURE.

Previously used exclusively as an energy crop, the fibers of the silphia plant can now be used as a new raw material in paper production.

Pulpwood is still the preferred base in paper production today. By the time the wood cellulose finds its way to paper production or the manufacturing of other pulp products, it has gone through numerous energy and chemical intensive processes. At the same time, the need for the delicate resource, wood, increases constantly. That is why alternatives to conventional production are more in-demand than ever before. With the production of natural fibers from the silphia plant, from the family Asteraceae, and their use in the manufacturing of paper and other fiber-based products, OutNature has developed an innovative method. The fiber alternative is already used at a minimum of 35 percent in paper quality and successfully helps to lead the in-demand material into the future.

The brand OutNature was founded in 2019 as a start-up belonging to the PreZero family of companies, the environmental division of the Schwarz Group. Using their own technology, OutNature aims to create an economical and ecological fiber alternative for paper and packaging manufacturing. OutNature is designed to not only significantly reduce the use of conventional pulp via the partial use of the silphia alternative, but also to promote independence from the volatile global pulp market.

The process for extracting the fibers from the plant, up until now primarily used in the production of biogas, doesn't use much energy and only requires small amounts of water. The leftover plant components can continue to be used as fermentation substrate.

In addition to that, OutNature would like to establish a circulatory system based on the processing of the silphia plant, which would regionalize paper production across the entire creation process. From the cultivation and the logistics, to the paper production and packaging manufacturing, to commerce and the subsequent disposal and recycling, OutNature Paper wants to think in new ways and put down roots in their manufacturing region. With an innovative, bio-economic solution approach, they aim to succeed in permanently strengthening rural areas and creating jobs, while at the same time providing comprehensive, "Made in Germany" value creation. OutNature wants to design efficient solutions for commerce and industry that also contribute to a stable and sustainable future.

The paper manufactured on the basis of the silphia plant possesses an especially natural look and feel. With merchandise displays in German retail stores, as well as the introduction of silphia packaging for organic products from the private labels of Kaufland and Lidl, OutNature has already been able to demonstrate its versatile applications in practice. Becoming certified according to the FSC standard, holding the ISEGA certificate for food contact materials and other certifications, as well as proof of recyclability, have created the foundation for further possible applications and have paved the way into the market for OutNature. Their evolution has been accompanied by numerous awards such as the German Packaging Award 2020, the German Design Award 2022, the German Innovation Award 2022, the World Star Packaging Award 2021 and the Bio-Economic Innovation Award BW 2020.

FACTS AND FIGURES

PRODUCTS
sustainable fiber and paper products based on the silphia plant for packaging solutions in commerce and industry

LOCATION
Neckarsulm, Baden-Württemberg

FOUNDER
OutNature is a brand belonging to the environmental service provider PreZero (Schwarz-Group)

EMPLOYEES
14 (2022)

SALES
DACH-region; further internationalization currently being planned

WEBSITE
out-nature.de

SHADESIGN

SUN PROTECTION SYSTEMS

The classic awning is significantly outdated in terms of design. With the SHADE-Shadow-System, SHADESIGN connects innovative technology with a contemporary, stylish look.

PASSION FOR
SHADE

As a producer of sun protection systems and engineered fabrics, SHADESIGN GmbH, from the upper Bavarian city of Bruckmühl, has dedicated itself to the subject of sun protection with total entrepreneurial passion for more than half a century. SHADESIGN develops and produces awnings, fixed sails, and engineered fabrics, which offers retailers and customers in architecture and construction a wide range of possibilities to integrate sun protection harmoniously into part of the building design.

Named for its founders, Mayle & Fellermeier GmbH in Kolbermoor near Rosenheim presented itself as the first manufacturer of high frequency welded, coated PVC cloths. Truck tarpaulins and awning fabrics helped the business achieve steady growth. After its current owner, Florian Aulinger took over, the strategic focus on the product area of sun protection followed step by step starting in 1995.

Since 2012, the SHADE-Shadow-System has been the core product at the heart of the enterprise. The one-of-a-kind, internationally patented system consisting of modular, expandable shade solutions offers reliable and almost limitlessly combinable sun protection as well as comfortable rain protection in various configurations. The innovative strength of the 50 employees of the company, which was consequently renamed SHADESIGN GmbH in 2018, doesn't only encompass the work of the sailmakers and fabric manufacturing technicians. As part of its international orientation, product design is also becoming increasingly important, with the introduction of and focus on the SHADE rollable sail. The entire collection distinguishes itself not only through its user-friendly easy operability but also through its purist "cool" look. The design isn't only well-received by its customers, as proven by the German Design Award in 2021, which honored the SHADE-Shadow-System as an "Excellent Product Design" in the category "Gardening and Outdoor Living."

Running parallel to the focus on the SHADE shadow system is the growth of the international engagement of the Bavarian manufacturer since 2018. The sales team was significantly expanded under the new CEO, Frank Reisenauer, and in 2020 the marketing, e-commerce, and social media divisions were restructured following their takeover by Silvia Reh. The responsibility for the critical expert view of the market environment has been taken on by the new product manager, Christian Simon, also since 2020.

The key to success has proven to be the collective vision of every employee. SHADESIGN's first priority is quality and service, which is the basis for

developing a close, trustworthy, and reliable collaboration within the company as well as in exchange with its partners. A fair and open working atmosphere is equally a fundamental part of the company's philosophy, as well as dealing responsibly with aspects such as sustainability, with a view to in-house production as well as during the selection of suitable suppliers and subcontractors.

FACTS
AND FIGURES

PRODUCTS
awnings, fixed sails,
engineered fabrics

LOCATION
Bruckmühl, Bavaria

FOUNDERS
Gerhard Mayle and Anton Fellermeier
(1964, Kolbermoor, as G. Mayle &
A. Fellermeier GmbH)

OWNER
Florian Aulinger

MANAGING DIRECTORS
Florian Aulinger
Frank Reisenauer

EMPLOYEES
50 (2022)

SALES
B2B to specialist retailers,
90 percent in the DACH region,
10 percent in export countries

WEBSITE
shadedesign.de

Cloer

ELECTRICAL AND
SMALL KITCHEN APPLIANCES

The business group Caspar Cloer from Neheim on the Ruhr is
the market leader in the field of waffle irons. In 2023, the family
business will celebrate its 125th company anniversary.

Left photo: Safety, durability, and performance: quality checks in the Cloer in-house development laboratory.
Right photo: Cloer Lunch Care System: all the elements necessary for the convenient storage, transport, and reheating of your own meals on the go.

A brand with heart: this is not only reflected in the taste experience in the form of a heart, but also throughout the history of the company. Caspar Cloer founded his factory for electric heating and cooking appliances in 1898 in Neheim on the Ruhr (Arnsberg, South Westphalia). Driven by the new possibilities generated by electricity at the time, Cloer came up with the idea of the innovation of an electric waffle iron based on his flat iron production and was one of the first manufacturers to produce these appliances. Next, he experimented with various baking tins for flat cones and soft, cake-like waffles. In order to achieve the best taste experience for his waffles, he designed a symmetrical heart — which is how the iconic form of the Cloer-waffle with the pyramid cuts was created.

Thanks to continual advancement and the development of new product categories, the founder's last name has evolved over the following decades into a well-known brand. The product offering has since expanded to include everything from coffee machines and electric kettles, toasters and egg cookers, as well as barbeque and raclette grills and a lunch care system. The characteristic design element of the Cloer waffle machine — a large black handle, which closes the appliance — is constantly reinterpreted in the design language of further products and thus contributes to the brand's recognizability.

The in-house development laboratory plays an important role at Cloer headquarters in Neheim: there, groundbreaking products are put to the test for the current and future market. Mass productions take place at highly modern plants in Asia; sales take place via specialist stores and retail stores, as well as online in many countries worldwide.

In 2023, the fourth-generation family business will celebrate its 125th anniversary. Loyal to the motto: "Times change. The heart remains.," they focus on a lean production with fully digitalized business processes, as well as continual improvement of manufacturing and logistics; this is in order to guarantee the high quality of their products in terms of safety, durability, and performance to their customers. This is achieved not least through their own training of the employees of tomorrow, who often remain loyal to the company for decades, and make a decisive contribution to the high quality of the Cloer brand.

FACTS AND FIGURES

PRODUCTS
electrical and small kitchen appliances

LOCATIONS
headquarters in Neheim on the Ruhr,
multiple production facilities in Asia

FOUNDER
Caspar Cloer (1898, Neheim)

OWNERS
the fourth generation of the Cloer family

EMPLOYEES
50 employees worldwide

SALES
in numerous countries worldwide
via specialty and retail stores as well
as online

WEBSITE
cloer.de

HAILO-Werk

METAL INDUSTRY

As the "Brand of the Century," HAILO looks back on a long, successful history. The company began to connect innovation, quality, and strategic brand development early on.

Since 1953 HAILO has focused on innovative waste bin solutions for the kitchen

FACTS AND FIGURES

PRODUCTS
ladders/ladder systems and trash systems/waste bins

LOCATIONS
Haiger, Hessen
subsidiaries in France, Czech Republic and USA

FOUNDERS
Rudolf und Irene Loh
(1947, Haiger)

OWNER
Sebastian Loh

EMPLOYEES
460 (2022)

SALES
worldwide

WEBSITE
hailo.de

During the course of three generations, the HAILO company has succeeded in making a name for itself internationally over 75 years — literally. The combination of the location where the business was founded, HAIger, and the name of the couple who founded it, Rudolf and Irene LOh, created the base for the brand HAILO, which has been established today in households as well as in a professional context. When it comes to ladders and waste bins, the company's core products, there is no way for customers in the B2B and B2C areas to not have noticed HAILO. The distinctive design of HAILO products contributes to its brand awareness and is highly recognizable due to its color scheme and consistent use of characteristic, functional design elements. Ladders, for example, can be identified as HAILO brand products at first glance due to their striking red hinges. In combination with innovative product development and high quality standards, HAILO has managed to attain international prominence and successfully hold their own among the competition.

The push to consistently develop the HAILO brand was initiated by Joachim Loh, son of the founder and father of the current holder, Sebastian Loh. During his time as managing director, which began in 1971, the brand logo was developed — only slightly different today than the original version — and the fundamental principles of their corporate identity were created and implemented.

HAILO unites three independent divisions with varied target groups under one brand. HAILO home & business features ladders and steps as well as waste bins for working in the home and garden. HAILO Einbautechnik combines diverse built-in solutions for waste bins and organizational systems for the kitchen industry. The third division, HAILO Professional, offers innovative access and safety technology for building construction and civil engineering. In addition to the brand name, the three divisions are united by a common brand identity: HAILO stands for ease of use, top quality, and safety.

During more than seven decades of company history, HAILO has been successful as a family-owned company in aligning itself with changing market conditions and evolving and establishing the brand HAILO. With digitalization, especially in the area of data management, HAILO took another step into the future of the brand during the corona pandemic. On the basis of the gathered data and information about their customers, products, and services, today HAILO works on needs-based innovations which are guiding the brand into the future, and making the company more resilient for any coming challenges.

HAILO ladder-system expertise can also be found in underground construction.

63

QLOCKTWO

ARTISTIC TIMEPIECES

Time in a new dimension: QLOCKTWO is aesthetic timepieces made with great craftsmanship.

Time is mystery created by humanity. Only understanding it through language has given it its unique meaning. QLOCKTWO transforms the clock from a classic display of time to an object of applied art, where the time is shown through a matrix of letters in written words. The surfaces of the luxurious timepieces can be varied in different colors and materials. These include natural slate, 24 karat gold leaf, pure platinum, rusted or raw steel as well as patinaed copper. Furthermore, QLOCKTWO is available in more than 20 languages and dialects.

The basis of their creative concept is an intensive artistic exploration of the theme of time since the 1990s. Biegert and Funk have created a totally new product category through QLOCKTWO, which possesses a clearly unique selling point and an extensive copyright with 23 patents to date in different countries. Together with the founders, the managing partner Jens Adamik is responsible today for the brand and the development of the business. As the first multimedia trademark to be registered in Germany, QLOCKTWO connects the principle of time measurement with handcrafted art and modern interior design. QLOCKTWO is available in different dimensions and designs.

Over the years, these unique timepieces have won more than 30 design awards and are represented in the collection of the Württemberg State Museum as national treasures. The commitment to Germany as a business location is an important part of the company philosophy: the QLOCKTWO manufacturer is located in Schwäbisch Gmünd, the hometown of the designers. Suppliers come from the surrounding area in order to keep delivery distances shorter and to strengthen jobs in the region. During the creation and refinement of the unique pieces, industrial manufacturing techniques are complemented by the finest craftsmanship of highly skilled artisans.

In a world that continues to get more and more complex, these unique timepieces fulfill the human need for clarity and calm, together with a moment of conscious deceleration. QLOCKTWO invites you to take a break from the fast pace of daily life, pause, and develop a new feel for time.

FACTS AND FIGURES

PRODUCTS
artistic timepieces

LOCATIONS
Germany, Switzerland, USA

FOUNDERS
Marco Biegert and Andreas Funk

MANAGING DIRECTORS
Marco Biegert, Andreas Funk and Jens Adamik

EMPLOYEES
60 (2022)

SALES
worldwide through exclusive specialty stores, their own single-brand stores, and online

WEBSITE
qlocktwo.de

QLOCKTWO®

65

3deluxe

ARCHITECTURE AND DESIGN

As a design and architecture firm, 3deluxe has assisted clients from industry, retail, and real estate, as well as private individuals. In countless award-winning projects both domestically and internationally, 3deluxe designs trendsetting, urban living spaces with mass appeal.

With a high level of specialist expertise and the interdisciplinary teamwork between architects, interior designers, landscapers, and designers, the design firm has been successful over the three decades since its founding in connecting the brand 3deluxe with impressive buildings, rooms, and installations.

As an entrepreneurial symbiosis between "3" company founders and the highest quality standards on a "deluxe" level, 3deluxe unites the various areas of competence transmedially, in the area of tension between architecture and design, art, and pop culture. This continues to produce unique projects, such as the multimedia theme world SCAPE in the context of the Expo 2000; the Cocoon Club in Frankfurt (2004); the scenography and the stage design including all constructions, as well as the costume and sound design for the approximately 10-minute-long closing ceremony at the FIFA WM 2006 on behalf of Andr. Heller; the Leonardo Glass Cube (2007) in Bad Driburg, used as a flagship showroom for the well-known eponymous manufacturer of drinking vessels and glass accessories. Equally worth mentioning are the Noor Island Park (2015), a transmedial stage-managed nature park in the United Arab Emirates; the Harting European Distribution Center (2019); the FC Campus (2020); the V-Plaza Lithuania (2020); and the #WeThePlanet Campus / Floating Platform (2021).

The countless international projects unite the trendsetting design approach, which integrates ecologically vulnerable aspects and focuses on people and nature equally. 3deluxe stands for an iconographic design vocabulary that contributes to a sense of well-being. That is how a historic plaza in Lithuania became the multi-award-winning V-Plaza, an urban living room and hybrid of peaceful green oases, water features, cafes, and modern office spaces.

The international perception of the consistently positive transformations of locations designed by 3deluxe has also been reflected in numerous awards. Noteworthy is, among others, the Green Good Design Award 2022. On behalf of the New York organization We The Planet and their concept of a green company building designed with people in mind, 3deluxe designed an urban habitat built on an existing flat roof. In doing so, 3deluxe followed the 50/50 principle, where the interior space used by people gives as much back to nature as it takes from it, which the concept incorporates interactively.

3deluxe views all its awards as additional motivation for its work with design experts, advanced technologies, and a resource-conserving use of materials.

FACTS AND FIGURES

PRODUCTS
architecture, interior, design

LOCATIONS
Wiesbaden, Miami, Dubai

FOUNDERS
Nik Schweiger, Andreas and Stephan Lauhoff, Dieter Brell (Wiesbaden, 1995)

OWNERS
Peter Seipp, Dieter Brell, Stephan and Andreas Lauhoff

EMPLOYEES
45 (2021)

SALES
global efficiency; partner network with developers, architects, and experts on site

WEBSITE
3deluxe.de

3DELUXE

Left: MERCK – eyrise® cubicle© by 3deluxe, 2021 \\ Photography: Sascha Jahnke; Right: V Plaza© by 3deluxe, 2020 \\ Photography: Norbert Tukaj

KISKA

BRANDS, DESIGN, AND COMMUNICATION

As an integrated consulting agency, KISKA uses the methodology of Integrated Design Development in order to create successful brands and to reposition and strengthen already established brands.

DESIGNING DESIRE

Strictly speaking, it is not difficult to found a company and bring a product out on the market. Maintaining the brand long-term on the market and elevating yourself above the competition — that, on the other hand, is a significant achievement. If you look at every company that has been able to maintain its success, in some cases over decades, what sets the company and its offering apart rapidly becomes clear: the combination of a relevant product with a unique brand experience.

Successful brands stand out primarily because of their recognizability, which results from a strategic, audience-oriented approach to design and communication. Developing both of these and being able to adapt to changing requirements and conditions in the long term demands creativity, expert knowledge and experience: all qualities that KISKA has developed over the past 30 years and has been able to successfully unite in their studio as an integrated consulting company.

KISKA supports global companies in the fields of mobility, sporting goods, consumer tech, and professional tools with services provided in the areas of branding, design and communication. KISKA uses the skills and resources of its total 250 employees in four studios to develop custom combinations. On behalf of their customers, KISKA creates brand-related product and service experiences in order to create brands, strengthen them or completely reposition them.

KISKA GmbH was founded in 1990 as an agency for product design by its eponymous founder, Gerald Kiska in Salzburg. Among the most well-known customers of the company to date is the motorcycle brand KTM, which has maintained a brand design partnership with KISKA since 1991, in the context of which KISKA was largely responsible for the popular two-wheeler design. Within the following years, KISKA was successful in gradually expanding its expertise, attracting new prestigious customers and growing its own company. As a result, KISKA had expanded its service portfolio by 2015 with the addition of the areas of communication design, mobility design, and digital design as well as research, brand consulting, product consulting, and clothing and shoe design.

With their move into a new, 6,000 square meter studio in Salzburg (2008), as well as the opening of more studios — in Murrieta, California (2015), Shanghai (2018), and Munich (2021) — KISKA is not only constantly expanding its entrepreneurial scope of action, but above all its competencies. Two hundred and fifty creative experts from more than 35 nations work together on an interdisciplinary level, and especially profit from the diversity of the team. They establish the corporate culture that is equally key to KISKA's success and the success of the brands that they create.

FACTS AND FIGURES

PRODUCTS
services in the areas of brand, design, communication

LOCATIONS
Salzburg (headquarters),
Munich, Shanghai, Murrieta

FOUNDER
Gerald Kiska
(1990, Salzburg)

OWNERS
Sébastien Stassin and Julian Herget
(Managing Partners),
Ferdinand Klauser (Partner and
General Manager of KISKA brand
Shanghai), Gerald Kiska
(Founder and Chairman)

EMPLOYEES
15 in Germany,
250 worldwide (2022)

WEBSITE
kiska.de

KISKA.

KISKA combines creative disciplines in order to develop new brands and strengthen established brands: everything under one roof.

OBJECT CARPET

TEXTILE FLOOR COVERINGS

OBJECT CARPET is in pursuit of a revolutionary business goal: conquest of the industry with the first circular carpeting. The company connects sustainability with award-winning design and an impressive variety of colors.

DESIGN
FOR RECYCLING

Design XPOSIVE from the PLACES OF ORIGIN collection | Photo: Andreas Hoernisch Photographie

"Made in Germany" for 50 years: that is what OBJECT CARPET stands for as specialists for carpeting in the property sector. The company, founded by Roland Butz in 1972 in the Baden-Württemberg town of Denkendorf and currently managed by the second generation, his son Daniel Butz, has created a name for itself in the German-speaking region and beyond due to its resilient, durable, and versatile (thanks to the surface structure and color variety) textile floor coverings.

Customized carpets in 1,200 colors and varied three-dimensional print designs offer commercial customers, architects, interior designers and office outfitters a range of options to combine durable floor coverings with custom design ideas and to create home and office spaces according to the wishes of their clients.

Since 2017, OBJECT CARPET has consciously focused on environmentally friendly and health-conscious production methods. With the introduction of the innovative process of WELLTEX® carpet backing, OBJECT CARPET is able to avoid using PVC, bitumen and latex throughout the entire tile collection and is even able to improve fundamental product features such as elasticity and installation convenience.

The pursuit of continuous, integral advancement has proven to be a consistent theme throughout the company history of OBJECT CARPET. In the year 2020, the company moved into their new headquarters in the architecturally noteworthy OBJECT CAMPUS. The innovative ensemble of buildings also connects design and sustainability and offers numerous businesses in addition to OBJECT CARPET optimal conditions for innovative work and cross-industry cooperation under the motto "City of Visions."

OBJECT CARPET further strengthened its market position in 2021 with the integration of its affiliated company TOUCAN-T and is focused on the meaningful and sustainable synergy between the two strong brands. Following the recent fusion of the two companies, a transparent factory in Krefeld has opened its doors in order to offer customers a more in-depth view of the variety of products and their production methods, in addition to the showrooms in Stuttgart, Berlin, Frankfurt, Hamburg, Munich, Zurich and Vienna.

Under the motto, "DESIGN FOR RECYCLING – FOREVER YOUNG," and with the launch of the first circular carpets, OBJECT CARPET continues to chase the ambitious goal of making an important contribution to environmental protection through cross-company and cross-industry knowledge transfer and cooperation. Without sacrificing quality, OBJECT CARPET has man-

The prestigious entrance area at the OBJECT CAMPUS | Photo: Markus Guhl

aged to produce carpets that are 100 percent recyclable or already made from recycled polyamide yarn (ECONYL® from Aquafil). In addition, adhesives made from similarly recyclable polyester are used, forgoing other fillers or common, often problematic ingredients.

FACTS AND FIGURES

PRODUCTS
textile floor coverings, carpets

LOCATIONS
Denkendorf (headquarters), Krefeld (manufacturing), Showrooms in Munich, Frankfurt am Main, Hamburg, Berlin, Zürich (CH), Vienna (AT)

FOUNDER
Roland Butz
(1972, Denkendorf)

OWNERS
Roland Butz, Daniel Butz (CEO)

EMPLOYEES
180 (2022)

SALES
B2B to architects, interior designers, builders, project developers, planners, office outfitters, interior decorators

WEBSITE
object-carpet.com

OBJECT CARPET

OBJECT CARPET × Ippolito Fleitz Group collection | Photo: Monica Menez

DESIGNTEAM | studiokurbos

studiokurbos GmbH

FULL-SERVICE DESIGN DEVELOPMENT

studiokurbos is an independent and owner-operated design studio with locations in Stuttgart and Shanghai. Its portfolio with a focus on the automotive industry is unparalleled in Germany.

As an interdisciplinary design partner, studiokurbos designs cars, products, and user interfaces for brands and markets all over the world.

Emotional storytelling distinguishes the designs of studiokurbos. Every client has specific requirements, wishes and expectations. The highly specialized design team from Stuttgart gets to the root of these expectations in order to develop overall concepts that are tailored and innovative for a brand. What will move people in the future is one of their central themes.

"We create physical as well as digital interactions that make the product or technology tangible for people in the truest sense of the word and which can be experienced in dialogue," said studio founder Andreas Kurbos. Each of his projects begins with a blank piece of paper and a clear mission. Clearly formulated goals form the foundation, which is why he creates the specific goals together with the client, in order to create strong identities based on them for the future. Over the course of the development process, the vision grows until the idea becomes visible, triggers emotion, and the interaction can be experienced. A design like that leaves a lasting mark on brands and companies.

In concept modelling, a sense of form, design understanding, and extensive experience in CAS are essential.

FACTS
AND FIGURES

PRODUCTS
full-service design services
with a focus on automotive

LOCATIONS
Stuttgart, Shanghai

FOUNDER
Andreas Kurbos
(2013, Stuttgart)

OWNER
Andreas Kurbos

EMPLOYEES
35 in Germany,
15 in China (2022)

SALES
Europe, Asia

WEBSITE
kurbos.com

studiokurbos

From the strategy and the first sketches to show cars and prototypes for the automobile industry: studiokurbos offers future-oriented design development as a full service. Clients include companies from the auto industry as well as technology concerns, medium-sized businesses and start-ups. In addition to mobility design, studiokurbos offers product design and user interface as well as user experience design.

In the wake of new technology, design development has gotten more and more complex. It is no longer enough to just choose materials and colors. Today, advanced knowledge is required, particularly in a situation where materials need to be used in the interior of a car that have self-disinfecting capabilities. The team of experts provide clients with support and advice throughout the entire development process, whether it be about sustainability, digitalization, surface design or virtual reality.

Andreas Kurbos founded the studio in the year 2013; the company's name is derived from his name. Just four years later, the first Chinese clients came to studiokurbos and many ground-breaking projects were created. In 2021, the designers won multiple design prizes and awards; among others being named by the German Design Council as, "Team of the Year '21."

The Stuttgart designer's method of operating continues to become more custom and agile. In close cooperation with the design studio in Shanghai, which was founded during the pandemic, they are able to serve a much wider field of clients. "The economic situation during the pandemic forced us to think differently and create space for new structures," Andreas Kurbos explained. "The result is a team that wasn't only able to hold on to its camaraderie, but strengthen it; amazing new projects that demand more from our designers and motivate them; and a shift in flexibility in all respects." In 2023, studiokurbos will celebrate its ten year anniversary.

To realize ideas, the design teams work together with various model construction partners.

Resilience is an in-demand strength, particularly when external factors disturb stability and predictability.

LUTZ DIETZOLD

BYOK

DESIGN-ORIENTED LIVING AND
PROPERTY LIGHT PRODUCTION,
LIGHT PLANNING

With boldness and flexibility, BYOK has developed timeless, high-quality, elegant, well-proportioned, exciting product solutions for nearly 25 years, that also reveal interesting details upon a second glance.

With the founding of their eponymous company in 1996, Kai and Catrin Byok proverbially made a virtue of necessity; after a design concept that the two had created was rejected by a lighting manufacturer, the product designer and the interior designer decided to take the fate of their careers into their own hands.

Since then, the pair and their team have developed residential lighting and lighting solutions for property and office use. The BYOK design is characterized by timeless elegance and a unique combination of form and light.

In the first years after its founding, the young company concentrated on sales via select retail stores. However, it quickly succeeded in winning over well-known clients as well. With architectural commissions from clients such as BMW, Porsche, Deutsche Bank, Kühne+Nagel, Rolex, Tesa, Festo, and numerous others, BYOK was able to rapidly surpass the economic results of its first years many times over.

On behalf of their customers, BYOK develops lighting solutions for exclusive villa developments, for office buildings, high rise façades and entire shopping centers. With lighting products for the interior, such as the office standing lamp "Grado", BYOK has won numerous design awards, from the Aluminum Award to the Bundesdesignpreis (German Design Award).

In addition to their focus on lighting products and solutions, BYOK knows how to adapt to changing market conditions and has expanded its portfolio to include other solution-oriented products, such as air disinfection units for architectural and office integration with a high-quality design appeal. In doing so, BYOK prefers to combine lighting with other trades and developed, for example, a fully mobile break room for the auto manufacturer Porsche in Leipzig. BYOK relies on a combination of in-house production and regional suppliers, depending on the project. With this strategy, BYOK has been successful in serving their customers individually, without economic constraints.

Now that the luxury segment has increasingly evolved into an important clientele in recent years, BYOK has understood how to adapt its corporate strategy to changing conditions and base the company and its services on topics such as sustainability, health and mindfulness. In addition, BYOK reconsidered its sales structure and strengthened its direct-to-consumer strategy.

FACTS AND FIGURES

PRODUCTS
Residential lighting and lighting solutions for property and office use, specialty lighting solutions, specialty lights, specialty product solutions, light planning

LOCATION
Rellingen near Hamburg

FOUNDERS
Kai and Catrin Byok (1996)

OWNERS
Kai and Catrin Byok

EMPLOYEES
26

SALES
Direct sales, Germany, the Netherlands, Belgium, Switzerland, Austria

WEBSITE
byok.lighting.com

BYOK

Beatthechamp
Flowarena

DESIGNER FOOSBALL TABLES

The Flowarena designer foosball table looks like a modern piece of furniture from the 1970s. It consists of high-quality materials and can be customized down to the smallest details.

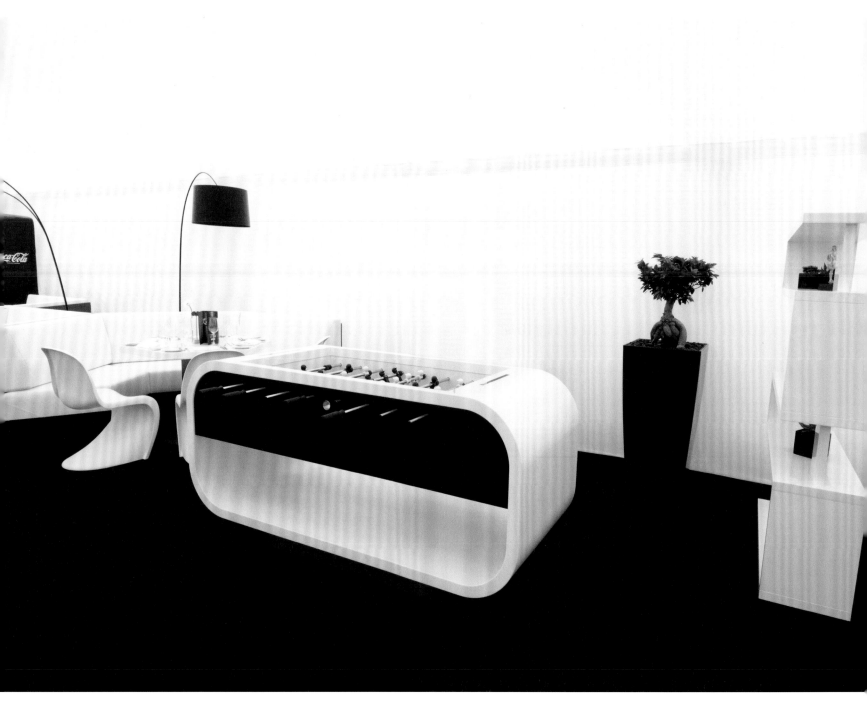

Table football world champion Chris Marks is the only German national player to have been a part of every previous world cup medallion win in the sport. He is the founder of the event agency, "Beat the Champ," from Nidderau in Hessen and designed the Flowarena designer foosball table, which combines the functionality of a foosball table with the optics of an elegant piece of furniture. Every model is produced down to the smallest detail according to the individual wishes of the customer, and is therefore truly one-of-a-kind.

The designer foosball table is reminiscent of the modern furniture of the 1970s thanks to its cubic form with rounded corners. It stands on an adjustable base made of stainless steel, and the body is made from solid wood that has been stained. The surfaces can be veneered or painted in colors from the RAL scale and can be modified with leather, metal or faux fur. The choice of material determines the look of the foosball table, from classically elegant to futuristic and extravagant. Every Flowarena table is handmade by experienced carpenters from Franconia, during roughly 150 hours of work. Because Marks' quality standards are very high, he depends on craftsmanship from Germany and uses only high-quality materials in environmentally friendly manufacturing processes for his production.

The Flowarena, just like the other four patented foosball tables from Chris Marks, is tournament quality. Included in the standard configuration are, among other features, a matte lacquered body, a height-adjustable base, a flush stainless steel scorekeeper, and a white playing field with digitally printed lines. Depending on the site of installation, additional features can be added such as LED lighting, a sound system for an MP3-player, a TV module or a playing field with a custom design, such as a company logo. It is ideally suited to be a visual highlight in bars and hotels, as well as agencies, shops, clubs, or events.

Twenty-five years of experience in table football sports contributes to the design when Chris Marks develops his foosball models. As the most important product of his company, "Beat the Champ," he calls the foosball table, "The Champ." He organizes exhibition appearances, kick-off events, client events or team building events for companies with his self-designed play tables. In his free time, Chris Marks works as a, "Laureus Ambassador" with social sports programs for children and teens.

FACTS AND FIGURES

PRODUCTS
designer foosball tables

LOCATION
Nidderau

FOUNDER
Chris Marks (2001, Beat the Champ, Nidderau)

OWNER
Chris Marks

EMPLOYEES
7 (cooperation partners abroad, 2022)

SALES
worldwide

WEBSITE
beatthechamp.de

BEAT THE CHAMP

in medias rees

The Stuttgart based advertising agency in medias
rees gets to the root of its client's USP. This is how
unique brand identities are created that are impressive, successful, and tell a story.

How do you make a brand bloom? With lots of commitment, passion and competence – the Stuttgart based advertising agency in medias rees delivers creative solutions which make brands and products on the market distinctive and therefore more successful. "Our USP is to find our client's USP," explained Simone Rees, founder and owner of the agency. Only then will an individualized concept to develop and maintain the brand be created. "We take the client seriously, listen to them, put them in the best light, and make them unparalleled among the competition."

At the beginning of every project is a strong idea, which gets implemented in a way that is visually appealing and intelligent in its content. The designer is sure that the success of a brand is inseparably connected to its aesthetic. "Good design takes this into account and prevents beauty from being reduced to mere decoration. Aesthetics communicate just as much about a business as facts and figures do. They appeal to our senses, evoke emotion, tell stories, linger in our consciousness and ensure the positive impact of a brand." Through new technology and digital transformation, brand design is subject to a permanent process of change. Simone Rees views that as a chance. Because of this, the oft-quoted principle for modern design, "form follows function," becomes for her a more contemporary, "beauty follows usability."

The name of the agency, in medias rees, is based on a play on words. Thanks to the last name of the founder, an "e" is added to the Latin expression which means, "in the middle of things." "We like to get to the heart of things and not let up until we have separated the wheat from the chaff. That's why we take so much time to do the fundamental research," emphasized Simone Rees. "Just like an onion, we remove layer after layer until we get to the center in order to find out what makes our clients special. The flower bulb is an integral part of our logo because we are convinced that every client already has their USP inside them and it only needs to be made visible."

A flexible network comprised of experienced specialists makes it possible for the agency to implement creative communication concepts and image campaigns in every sector and every channel. Her clients include design-oriented companies, from manufacturers to urban educational facilities. An intensive examination of zeitgeist, society, and cultural movements flow constantly into the design. This holistic method has been recognized with notable design awards. In 2022, in medias rees received the German Design Award for its innovative packaging concept for a new organic ice cream from Demeter, on behalf of the ice cream manufacturer Martosca. "Every brand identity looks completely different with us- and yet our signature is still always recognizable," said Simone Rees.

FACTS AND FIGURES

PRODUCTS
brands and communication design;
advertising

LOCATION
Stuttgart

FOUNDER
Simone Rees
(Stuttgart, 2002)

OWNER
Simone Rees

EMPLOYEES
2

SALES
Germany

WEBSITE
inmediasrees.de

IN MEDIAS REES.
WERBEAGENTUR

EIN LÖFFELCHEN FÜR DICH.   EIN LÖFFEL FÜR DIE WELT.

DAS GUTE EIS

83

Frescolori

MINERAL-BASED SMOOTHING COMPOUND

Walls, floors, and bathrooms with an elegant look: the product range of the brand Frescolori, from Bocholt, contains smoothing compounds with a mineral base that are very high-quality and robust.

The painting master Frank Ewering was not satisfied with the conventional smoothing compounds from Italy, which is why he created his own recipe with a mineral base more than 25 years ago. The product that came out of that is, "Frescolori," a combination of the Italian words "fresco," for fresh, and "colore," for color. As a third-generation painting master, he decided to be self-employed with his unmistakable base mix, which harmoniously united Italian wellness with German perfection. The products from the brand Frescolori contain almost exclusively natural substances, which combine seamlessly with each other during a four-day maturation process; the exact recipe remains, of course, a secret...

Today, the owner-operated business from the Münsterland city of Bocholt has diverse products in its range. "Caramor," is a unique base product: it consists of more than 96 percent natural materials, is breathable, and improves the climate of the room. The surface "structure" is advantageous because spots can be easily sanded away with a sanding pad. The recipe contains limescale substances in combination with just a trace of plastic. The limescale gives the surface a natural appearance, in contrast to cement and plaster. In comparison with clay, the limescale product is hard and robust. With "Puramente," bathrooms can be designed without seams, even with already laid tiles. "Maranzo," was developed for a seamless floor with an elegant look. This special compound has already proven itself

in highly frequented areas such as train station malls and hotels. And the spackled exposed concrete, "Frescoton" is a multi-award-winning design classic.

Even unusually creative solutions, such as metallic surfaces, are achievable thanks to the range of products. These sorts of solutions are used by architects, interior designers, and designers as well as painters and varnishers for the end-customer. The process is performed exclusively by certified workers who have already completed a course of training at Frescolori. The so-called limescale cycle illustrates the process of application: after the quarried limestone is fired, it gets extinguished and becomes a new product. When it dries, it turns back into limestone and is therefore especially robust. Small containers are also used in order to create less waste that needs to be disposed of.

Over the course of 30 years, Frescolori has evolved from a one-man painting service to a manufacturer with 40 employees for high-quality and creative surface finishes. The company constantly renews its structures and transforms its processes, in order to retain a strong presence on the market. The second generation is already working as well, and developing new ideas such as a furniture collection with surfaces from Frescolori. Among the references of the family-owned company are imposing projects such as a 30,000 square meter wall design in a bank building in Frankfurt am Main.

FACTS AND FIGURES

PRODUCTS
mineral based smoothing compound

LOCATION
Bocholt, Münsterland

FOUNDER
Frank Ewering (1993, Bocholt)

OWNERS
the Ewering family

EMPLOYEES
40 (2022)

SALES
worldwide; distributors for the Netherlands, France, Switzerland, and Taiwan

WEBSITE
frescolori.de

PURAMENTE is perfectly suited for wet rooms, as it is water resistant and very low-maintenance.

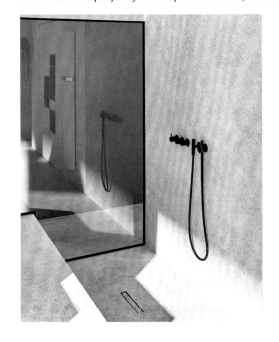

bk Group AG

THE EXPERTS FOR STORE BUILDING AND TECHNICAL FACILITY MANAGEMENT, DESIGNED BY THE BK WORLD, THE FUTURE OF MOBILITY.

"What if customers could have one single provider for the complete interior fitting, and for all maintenance tasks, related to their property, in a manner that would enable them to concentrate exclusively on their core business?" This idea, from Gerold Wolfarth, was the initial impulse for the foundation of the bk Group, which followed in 1999, and is still the foundation for their business model today.

b k stands for "baukreativ" (build creative). That is what the company was called in its original form. The bk Group develops and implements sustainable and innovative interior construction projects and offers the planning, construction, and maintenance of retail stores, car dealerships, or fitness studios for clients throughout all of Europe. All of their services come from a single source. The client base of the bk Group AG includes international brands such as Rituals, Prada, Guess, Hunkemöller, Swarovski, Hermès, and many more.

What began as a start-up quickly became the leading general contractor for property construction and facility management. Due to the strong growth and diversification of the company, the bk Group AG was formed as an umbrella company.

The lockdown in 2020 took 100 percent of the work foundation away from the business group. As a result, the management decided to pursue new avenues in order to ensure that the company would remain fit for the future. That is how the bk World concept was born. For its world premiere on June 3, 2022, the first gas station of the future was opened in Endsee, Bavaria, in cooperation with TESLA.

This sustainable layover-lounge, at an electric car charging park, is made of hyperflexible room elements that are climate positive and made from solid spruce-wood. As it is a modular system, it is able to grow with the charging park. The rooms can be constructed and deconstructed flexibly, transported, and need only water, sewage, and electricity. Because of that, they can be placed on previously undeveloped locations. A faster construction of the electric car charging network is actively supported.

In the so-called "Qubes," waiting time for drivers of electric cars becomes quality time: the lounge, modern sanitary facilities, offices, a children's play area, healthy food and drinks, as well as a connection to the bk World online shop, where regional retailers can sell their products. With this in-depth sustainability approach, as well as its diverse offering, bk World is internationally one-of-a-kind.

The design is modern and comfortable, the futuristic shape immediately attracting attention. The highly efficient design incorporates an extremely large number of offerings on a comparatively small footprint. Over the next five years, the company plans to open 300 more locations in Europe for various charging park operators and is therefore actively shaping a trend that will lead the company securely into the future.

FACTS AND FIGURES

PRODUCTS
planning, construction, and maintenance of retail stores

LOCATIONS
Headquarters in Endsee, Bavaria.
Subsidiaries in Berlin and Düsseldorf.
Offices in Paris, London, Stockholm, Budapest, Milan and Barcelona.

FOUNDER
Gerold Wolfarth
(Founder and CEO since 1999),
Managing Director is Marc Arnold.

OWNER
Gerold Wolfarth

EMPLOYEES
250 (2022)

SALES
Europe-wide with an employee network of permanently employed service technicians in the different countries.

WEBSITE
bk-group.eu

Credit: bk World Holding GmbH

VOLA

PLUMBING

VOLA has been a trendsetter for fittings and
accessories for plumbing and kitchens since 1968.
Since then, VOLA has established itself as a modern,
international brand with traditional values.

The VOLA modular system.

W here design meets essential everyday objects, the combination of practical utility and design has proven to be particularly noteworthy. Plumbing fittings in the bathroom and kitchen primarily have a practical function; the product design contributes largely to functionality and comfort of use but is still an important element of the decorative and therefore emotional added value.

With an unchanged classic design, the Danish brand VOLA has set the standard in the field of plumbing design for more than 50 years. The sink fittings HV1 and the single lever mixer KV1 are viewed today as timeless design classics. The KV1 owes its inclusion in the design collection of the MoMA in New York, as well as numerous other design awards, to its iconic form.

At the beginning of their collaboration, company founder Verner Overgaard and designer Arne Jacobsen paid attention to not only the visual appearance, but combined it with innovative plumbing technology to achieve VOLA's present-day characteristic purist design. With the VOLA 111 model, Jacobsen and Overgaard succeeded in developing the world's first concealed fitting during a competition held by the Danish National Bank and with that, started a trend that has been successfully implemented in bathrooms around the world today.

The company has seamlessly continued the success of those first years with a continuous expansion of their product range. In doing so, VOLA, which still manufactures exclusively in Denmark, has continued to set new trends through a diversity of materials and color schemes. VOLA was the first company worldwide to bring color into bathrooms and kitchens and offers their fittings in varied finishes and colors today.

VOLA fittings are found all over the world, not only in private bathrooms and kitchens but also in hotels, airports, and cultural institutions. VOLA is not only compelling in terms of design; from the beginning, the company has also continuously focused on the most modern technology and durability. VOLA fittings can be put together individually from separate components according to a basic modular principle. In combination with the variety of colors, this offers private as well as corporate customers the ability to customize the design. The modular design system combines different fittings with levers, plates, and outlets. In addition to the immense amount of options, the modular system also offers obvious advantages in terms of maintenance and repair. VOLA fittings are straightforward to repair through the replacement of individual components and are therefore significantly more durable than standard fittings.

This is how VOLA has succeeded in growing over the decades, continuously evolving while still maintaining their principles of success.

FACTS AND FIGURES

PRODUCTS
fittings and accessories for plumbing and kitchens

LOCATIONS
Denmark (parent company), subsidiaries worldwide

FOUNDER
Verner Overgaard
(1968, Horsens/Dänemark)

OWNERS
the Overgaard family

EMPLOYEES
300 (2022)

SALES
direct sales, sales through subsidiaries and commercial agencies

WEBSITE
vola.com

Left: The design classic, modern and groundbreaking since 1968.
Right: The VOLA classic KV1 gleams in the new PVD color gold.

markilux

AWNINGS

For more than 50 years, the modern family business markilux, from Emsdetten in Münsterland, has developed high quality sun protection solutions. Their story was born from the spirit of innovation, growth, and their employees' commitment. Every product created by the specialists for designer awnings impresses with its quality and durability, optical elegance and a high degree of utility for discerning clients from different industries in Germany as well as worldwide.

The product range today encompasses awnings for the patio, windows and sunrooms, and free-standing awnings as well as large area shading for spacious gardens, restaurants, hotels, businesses or cafés. There is also an exclusive collection of awning cover fabrics, designed by markilux and woven at the same location by its sister company.

Aside from high quality and stylish design, it is also important to the company that the awnings have a long lifespan. They are produced to last a small "eternity" and therefore set themselves apart from the many short-lived products of today. There is also no stock manufacturing at markilux: every awning is unique, tailor-made to order; this provides their customers with lots of options to custom-design their sun and wet weather protection.

One of the main guiding principles at markilux is to continually perfect products and to give every awning an unmistakable, markilux-typical brand image, which unites design and technology, aesthetics and innovative function.

The business has consistently proven its courage in trying out new things. They are always experimenting with materials, form, and function. This has enabled the company to repeatedly set innovative trends in the industry and to occupy a leading position in the market. The goal is clear: to create awning designs that have enough potential to generate design classics.

For this reason, a markilux awning must match the aesthetic of contemporary architecture and ideally become a highlight of the house. This is made possible through closely observing the market, a creative development team, experimenting with exciting materials and surfaces as well as the motivation to continue reinterpreting awnings in their form. The awning cover fabrics are also important, as present and effective textile color surfaces that help shape the overall appearance of the awning should be timeless, but also trendy. The look of the awnings is coherent and coordinated with furniture, garden, and home style.

Change becomes a chance: in a time of intelligent production facilities, markilux has set a digital course. Many of the processes are already computer controlled. "Lifelong learning," and the constant willingness to question themselves and improve is another guiding principle at markilux. A program rewards employees for bringing in ideas about the processes in production and administration.

The brand has become recognized worldwide due to their successful philosophy, has won numerous awards and is ideally positioned to handle future challenges.

FACTS AND FIGURES

PRODUCTS
outdoor sun protection

LOCATIONS
Emsdetten (production facility); Sales locations via subsidiary companies in Salzburg, Madrid, London, Switzerland, France and Italy; affiliated companies in New York City and Sydney

FOUNDER
Carl-Hinderich Schmitz (1972)

OWNER
Holding Schmitz-Werke GmbH + Co. KG

MANAGING DIRECTORS
K. Wuchner and M. Gerling

EMPLOYEES
permanent employees: 350; seasonal employees: approx. 150 per year

SALES
private customers, restaurants, hotels, businesses in Germany and worldwide

WEBSITE
markilux.com

THE BEST UNDER THE SUN.
FOR THE MOST ALLURING SHADE
IN THE WORLD.

markilux

markilux awnings create stylish living spaces for patios and gardens

Mercedes-Benz Group AG

PREMIUM AND LUXURY CARS AND VANS

The new edition of an icon: the new luxury sportscar from the Mercedes Benz subsidiary Mercedes-AMG continues to write the success story of the SL-Class.

Approximately 70 years ago, the history of a sportscar that immediately became a legend began with public test drives: the first Mercedes racing car in the SL class, which was also roadworthy. Thanks to its success on international racetracks, the SL (short for super light) was quick to become legendary. The successful sportscar was followed in 1954 by the 300 SL series production sportscar, with its characteristic gullwing doors. A further highlight in the history of the model is the "Pagode," which was made from 1963 to 1971. From the very beginning up until today, the SL legend has been perpetuated in a manner typical for its time.

"We have achieved the rebirth of the iconic SL design with the new Mercedes-AMG SL. The expressively shaped exterior conveys a light and pure impression and brings sensual beauty and extravagant design into perfect harmony," said Gorden Wagener, Chief Design Officer Mercedes-Benz Group AG.

In the luxury sportscar segment, the new Mercedes-AMG SL has set the standard with its exciting design of sensual clarity, the most modern technology, and outstanding driving characteristics. The exterior design fascinates thanks to a perfect triad: it combines the modern Mercedes-Benz design philosophy of sensual clarity with the typical AMG sportiness and characteristic details. The two powerdomes on the hood are just one of numerous reminiscences from the first SL generation. The interaction between light and shadow make the overall image visually light. So, it is clear from first glance that the

new SL has gone back to its sporty roots. The interior of the new Mercedes-AMG SL has transformed the tradition of the first 300 SL Roadsters into a modern, high-end luxury design. Precious materials, meticulous finishes and a love for details also underline the high demand for luxury in the interior. The cockpit design, including the adjustable electric central display in the middle console, is focused on the driver and is compelling with its overall harmonious impression. The fully redesigned interior dimensions with 2+2 seating offers more function, as well as more space in the interior. The MBUX infotainment system offers several specific display styles and different modes to choose from.

FACTS AND FIGURES

PRODUCTS
premium and luxury cars and vans

LOCATION
Stuttgart, headquarters

FOUNDERS
Gottlieb Daimler (1883, Stuttgart),
Carl Friedrich Benz (1886, Mannheim)

CHAIRMAN OF THE BOARD
Ola Källenius

EMPLOYEES
172,000 (2022)

SALES
worldwide

WEBSITE
mercedes-benz.com

Mercedes-Benz

rational einbauküchen

KITCHEN INDUSTRY

One-of-a-kind kitchen design, which inspires so much more than just cooking: rational creates fitted kitchens whose design and functionality transform the kitchen into a modern and customized center of life.

With high-quality, premium fitted kitchens for every interior style, rational einbauküchen solutions have delighted not only proven hobby cooks for nearly six decades. Aside from the high standard of quality, which was rated at "good" and "very good" by the Stiftung Warentest as early as 1990, rational consciously changes with the times and views the modern kitchen as a multifunctional room. For this reason, the well-known maxim, "form follows function," has become increasingly meaningful for the kitchens from rational, especially as it relates to the combination of elegant designs with innovative and flexible functionality. The philosophy of viewing a kitchen as more than just a room to cook in is documented by rational einbauküchen solutions with their brand campaign under the slogan, "rational – so much more than a kitchen." Through this, rational integrates important subjects for the future such as sustainability and environmental and climate protection. The fact that the company clearly stands out from the competition in this respect is evidenced by the German Brand Award, which rational received again in 2022 after winning in 2021 and 2018 previously.

Multifunctionality and consumer-relevant subjects such as durability, trustworthiness, security, authenticity and naturalness have the same amount of value to rational einbauküchen solu-

tions as do questions of timeless design. In collaboration with designers like the multi-award-winning "popstar of the design world" Karim Rashid, rational designs fitted kitchen series' that hold their own over decades and are still able to remain current. The color scheme plays an important role here. rational einbauküchen solutions has been a member in COLORNETWORK® since 2022. The young manufacturer network has a special focus on product transparency and decides annually on a new color scheme, in addition to the "sustained color," which offers orientation and design freedom across product boundaries in interior design. The color selection guarantees long-term appeal as well as permanent combination possibilities and therefore sustainable value.

The identity of the brand rational einbauküchen solutions is the result of many years of continual further development. The company has consistently revisited its own strategy and adapted it to meet the current demands of the market, in order to remain in a good position for the markets of the future in the long term.

FACTS AND FIGURES

PRODUCTS
customized fitted kitchens

LOCATION
Melle, Lower Saxony

FOUNDER
Walter Fischer (1963, Melle)

OWNER
part of the international Bravat Group
since 2021

EMPLOYEES
62 (2022)

SALES
kitchen retailers worldwide

WEBSITE
rational.de

rational®

RATIONAL –
SO MUCH MORE
THAN A KITCHEN

A well-managed brand embodies the consumer's expectations of the company and its products, simplifies its orientation on the market, and conveys a feeling of security and stability.

PROF. MIKE RICHTER

Volkwagen ID.Buzz

Volkswagen

AUTOMOBILE

Volkswagen is among the largest auto manufacturers in the world and has shaped German automobile history. Volkswagen never viewed the subject of mobility as an end in itself, but as a fundamental necessity of humanity and society. This fundamental necessity has been further developed over time, and Volkswagen has provided an answer in the form of its family of models.

Volkswagen icons: Beetle, Golf I, ID.3

The Beetle initially stood for mass mobility and the freedom of travel for all. The Golf family, which stands for an entire generation, took the next step in 1974 and made new technology accessible for everyone. The Golf GTI can be seen as symbolical of this. And now, the ID. family again has the right answer at the right time; it heralds the arrival of the era of electric mobility and sustainability.

The success story of the Beetle began in 1938. The economical and affordable model mobilized and inspired the masses, and remained a bestseller and the most sold car in the world for decades, until it had to give the title to the VW Golf in 2002. It remained loyal to its pleasant, appealing, and functional design for years, reacting sensibly to social and technical developments. Through minute changes in the design alone, it was able to adapt its interior and exterior to changes in the zeitgeist and advancements in the automobile industry.

Since 1974, the Volkswagen Golf has represented innovation and the next great icon of automotive design with its minimalistic design and clear aesthetics; the engine was also moved from the trunk into the front of the car in this model. The Golf stands for safety, mobility, sincerity, and design for all — and is now in its eighth generation. The next major paradigm shift took place in 2019. Sustainability, a new awareness about the environment, life, and digitalization are all topics that move and change Volkswagen. One of Volkswagen's goals is e-mobility for everyone. The guiding principle, "Way to Zero," puts the environment at the center of their actions and is a sustainable influence on the design of the car.

The ID.3 is a part of the new ID. family and heralds the arrival of the age of electromobility. Just as with the first Beetle and the Golf I, the fully electricity powered car with compact dimensions stands for the beginning of an era. The design principles of the electric Volkswagen are marked by a new architecture, intelligence, and an experience for all the senses.

Volkwagen ID.B

Volkswagen Concept Car ID.AE

The ID. Buzz is the new face of sustainable mobility and creates a visual bracket around groundbreaking technology and functional design. "The T1 — an icon of the 1950s — made mobility and freedom possible for the people. With the ID. Buzz, we are transferring that T1 DNA into the present, and into the era of electromobility," described Jozef Kabaň, head of Volkswagen Design. "The ID. Buzz brings support and proximity to the people back to the street." The front section alone, with its graphic V, large logo, and friendly appearance, shows how much the ID. Buzz has revived the design-DNA of the T1. "We have developed an automobile layout with a logical and intuitive interior concept and a variable use of space. The interior can become a digital living room or office, just as our customers know it from home." And, as in the T1 before, this philosophy is clear to see in the linear dashboard with its calm, vertically stacked elements.

That design is no longer only about shape and styling is shown in the requirements of the ID. Buzz on the subject of sustainability: "We need to work on designing products that are long-lasting and sustainable, and offer an outstanding experience for our customers. On the

street, but also beyond it," said Jozef Kabaň. Leather and other animal-based products are completely avoided, and have been replaced by high-quality alternative materials with similar qualities and haptics. The seat covers, flooring, and ceiling upholstery in the ID. Buzz are made from recycled materials, among other things.

The ID. Buzz and the passenger car models of the ID. family are paving the way for the Volkswagen brand's ACCELERATE strategy and provide additional momentum toward e-mobility, software, and an expedited transition to a tech company. This is also reflected in the transformation of their headquarters in Wolfsburg, where roughly two billion euros are being invested into a new production facility in the immediate vicinity of the main plant.

In total, the company would like to invest more than 18 billion euros into electromobility, hybridization, and digitalization by 2026, in order to set standards in terms of fascinating digital customer experiences, new business models, and autonomous driving across the market. The vision: to turn Volkswagen into the most desirable brand for sustainable mobility.

FACTS AND FIGURES

PRODUCTS
automobile

LOCATIONS
30 locations in 13 countries

EMPLOYEES
180,000

SALES
car dealerships worldwide

WEBSITE
volkswagen.de

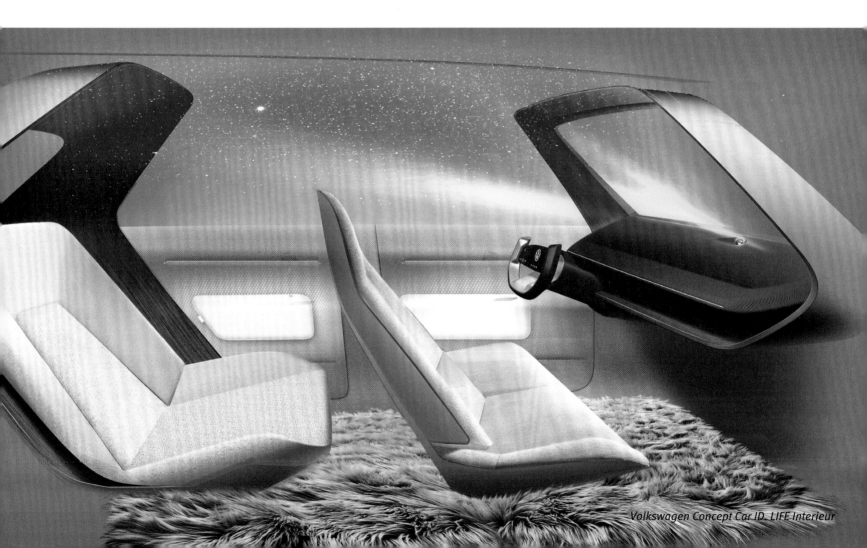

Volkswagen Concept Car ID. LIFE Interieur

KOTOAKI ASANO Architect & Associates

ARCHITECTURE, DESIGN, ART

Kotoaki Asano, born in 1972 in Tokyo, would like to create spaces where people can come together and relax. His architecture firm Asano Kotoaki, founded in 2005 in Yokohama, plans homes and other architectural projects, and designs spatial art and furniture. The architect and artist said of his work: "I am designing a part of the skin of the earth."

CREATING POETIC SPATIALITY

Credits: Yukio Yoshimura

Yukio Yoshimura

Kotoaki Asano

After his architectural studies at engineering school and his master's degree, which he completed in 1997 at the University of Tokyo, he worked from 1997 to 2005 at Hiroshi Hara + Atelier Φ in Tokyo before founding his own company. His architecture firm counts one employee: himself. He works with experts from various renowned construction companies during projects. His clients are private individuals as well as communes and organizations, such as a Japanese Christian church.

Many of his designs are aligned with the client's specifications as well as the conditions at their location; Kotoaki Asano is able to put more of himself into smaller buildings or his art. The rooms that he designs are intended to be individual and sensual, achieving a spatial visualization that transcends modernism. His signature and message are also meant to be conveyed. More than anything else, the architect tries to create a poetic space. He achieves this primarily through empty rooms that he integrates into his design and which are something, "poetic, ambiguous" for him.

This poetic nature is clear to see in his three main works: "Three Cubes in the Forest," "Gradation in the Forest," "Metamorphosis in the Forest."

The latter consists of the two areas "Gradation in the Forest," and "Three Cubes in the Forest." "Gradation in the Forest" is a collection of small rooms; "Three Cubes in the Forest" uses microarchitecture with various characteristics and functions and is easy to transport via truck. In the case of the collection, the rooms penetrate deeply into the forest; the house merges with nature. The three cubes appear as though they fell into the forest and spark curiosity about their interiors, which in turn creates an intriguing relationship between the interior and the surroundings and also a special perception of the forest.

Kotoaki Asano's architecture is inspired by the art and wood architecture from Europe and Japan. "In my designs of buildings and art I try to diminish the presence of the building, as in traditional Japanese architecture. I try to view architecture as something vague, like a cloud or fog, which merges with its surroundings," he described.

Kotoaki Asano has been honored with numerous national and international awards. In 2017 he received the iF Design Award in Hannover. In 2019, he was given, among others, the Architecture Master Prize 2019 in Los Angeles and was the Innovative Architecture winner of the ICONIC AWARD presented by the German Design Council. In the following year, he won the German Design Award, the Asia Design Prize, the Outstanding Property Award London, the DNA Paris Design Award, as well as the grand prize at the K-Design Award.

FACTS AND FIGURES

PRODUCTS
architectural design, spatial product design, room art

LOCATIONS
Tokyo and Yokohama (Japan)

FOUNDER
Kotoaki Asano (2005)

OWNER
Kotoaki Asano

SALES
Japan and other countries

WEBSITE
kotoaki-asano.com

KOTOAKI ASANO
Architect & Associates
浅野言朗建築設計事務所

POINTtec Products Electronic GmbH

WRISTWATCHES AND JEWELRY

The medium-sized company POINTtec has been independent and owner-operated for more than 30 years. High quality wristwatches with sophisticated custom designs are produced thanks to years of experience, a pioneering spirit and a sense of innovation. POINTtec watches stand for traditional craftsmanship, a long service life and an optimal price-performance ratio Made in Germany.

THE FINE ART OF
WATCHMAKING
MADE IN GERMANY

All designs are developed in the House of POINTtec and the watches are produced by highly qualified personnel in Germany, usually in the tradition-rich production facility in Ruhla in the Thuringia Forest. The product portfolio is multi-faceted: automatic watches in an entry-level price range, solar-powered watches, smart watches, and numerous classic series' with simple elegance.

Two series' have been inspired by aviation. For example, the dials in the collection IRON ANNIE play off of the corrugated metal structure of the legendary JU52 aircraft, making them distinctive pilot watches. In honor of the 100th birthday of the ZEPPELIN, POINTtec revived the glitz and glamour of the golden 1920s with an extraordinary women's watch. Just as with the Zeppelin airships, the watches from this collection are impressive in their technical refinement and timeless beauty. On the other hand, sports enthusiasts will find the right watch for every football moment in the series Kicker.

The collection has long included watches influenced by the Bauhaus style across brands. They were made to order in Ruhla — in a building now owned by POINTtec that was erected in 1929 according to designs based on Bauhaus principles by the renowned Jena architectural firm Schreiter & Schlag. "Bauhaus watches created in our own Bauhaus building – thanks to that, the history of our watches has become richer by a rather dazzling facet," company founder Willi Birk was pleased to say.

For many years, the company has produced high quality wristwatches according to their customer's wishes for well-known industrial companies, chain stores, distributors, and other outlets.

The newest series is the Sustainable Planet Edition, which meets the requirements of their sustainability project. The armband of the women's watch Grace is made from vegan leather, which is synthesized from 45 percent vegetable oils. The "Sustainable Planet" program was created to help innovative technologies, products, and companies gain more visibility. Also new in the collection is the POINTconnect smart band, a digital watchband with diverse functions such as notifications, activity tracking, health monitoring, navigation, Bluetooth, and much more. The band can be worn with your personal favorite watch and unites the traditional art of watchmaking with a digital future.

As a medium-sized company, it is important to POINTtec to analyze the latest trends and to continually evolve the company. The theme "recreate. transform. be resilient." resonates with the company's focus in many areas, from product development to sales and IT strategies.

By the way, the name POINTtec refers to the POINT and describes the motto of the company watches that get to the point. Numerous accolades from the German Brand Awards and the German Design Awards have validated the design concept and the company philosophy.

FACTS AND FIGURES

PRODUCTS
wristwatches

LOCATIONS
Ismaning and Ruhla

FOUNDER
Willi Birk,
(1987, Ismaning)

OWNERS
Nathalie Birk and Willi Birk

EMPLOYEES
approx. 50

SALES
in Germany through their own sales structure; sales representatives; retail stores, worldwide distributors in more than 30 countries

WEBSITE
pointtec.de

DALLMER

DRAINAGE SYSTEMS FOR HOME, GARDEN, AND PROPERTY

As a strong brand for drainage systems, Dallmer connects the latest technological advances with pioneering design and continually pushes the evolution of drainage further.

Innovative sanitary technology from Dallmer makes drainage in the home and on the property safe and convenient. The design concept takes on a high value during product development. This is because good design marries technical and creative know-how with user-oriented interests, according to the manufacturer from North Rhein Westphalian Arnsberg. In order to achieve this, Dallmer works successfully in interdisciplinary teams. Solutions are created through that varied expertise that question and reinterpret current standards and habits. Products with appealing forms and technical details that make them easy to install and meet all standards.

The "DallFlex" System for linear drainage was born out the idea of separating the shower channel from the drain, in order to have flexibility in installing level access showers. Its advantage is that the different shower channels are built on one and the same drain body. In addition to the "DallFlex" drain bodies, new types of channels have been added to the system that meet different design and budget requirements. Fine construction details make cleaning easier, improve hygiene, and optimize drainage.

On location in Arnsberg in Sauerland is where Dallmer manufactures its products as well as all necessary tools in house. In order to fulfill their high expectation of quality and precision, the family-owned company has developed its own processes and technologies. The goal of product development is to make the craftsmen's work as safe and easy as possible during installation. The manufacturer hires experts from multiple trade fields for this reason. This expertise contributes to Dallmer being one of the leading brands for drainage systems today.

Johannes Dallmer, Sr. founded the company in the year 1913 as a workshop for engraving and mold construction. His son, Helmuth, supplemented production with machines for thermoset and thermoplastic processing. In 1961, the first floor drain made of plastic was created, and two years later sanitary technology became a central division in the company. In the third generation, the design and technology enthusiast Johannes Dallmer took over the family business. Under his leadership, "CeraLine" was brought out onto the market in 2006, the first shower channel from Dallmer for the drainage of level-access showers in the bathroom. Today, Yvonne Dallmer leads the company from the fourth generation. Dallmer stands for innovative, award-winning design now more than ever, and has evolved into an "architect brand." With the current family of systems for point and linear drainage, "DallDrain" and "DallFlex," Dallmer has set the standard for the drainage of level-access showers and for many other drainage areas in the home.

The history of the company is characterized by continuous change. Through its willingness to question the familiar and remain open to the new, Dallmer has repeatedly succeeded in developing drainage technology that has permanently changed the industry. In doing so, design has played just as important a role as technology has.

FACTS AND FIGURES

PRODUCTS
drainage systems in the home and on the property

LOCATION
Arnsberg

FOUNDER
Johannes Dallmer Sr.

OWNERS
the third and fourth generations of the family

EMPLOYEES
233 (2022)

SALES
Europe, USA, Near and Middle East

WEBSITE
dallmer.de

DALLMER

Drainage technology from Dallmer makes unlimited design options possible.

DALI

HI-FI LOUDSPEAKERS

DALI loudspeaker systems set the highest standards for product development, sound enjoyment, and design. The flagship of the Danish company is the high-end series, "KORE."

A photo composition with the DALI RUBICON LCR loudspeaker for surround sound.

FACTS AND FIGURES

PRODUCTS
Hi-Fi loudspeakers for the stereo, home theater, and smart homes

LOCATIONS
Denmark, APAC countries, Benelux countries, Germany, Great Britain

FOUNDER
Peter Lyngdorf (1983, Nørager)

OWNER
Danish traditional company under private ownership

EMPLOYEES
290 (2021)

SALES
worldwide in approx. 70 countries

WEBSITE
dali-speakers.com

IN ADMIRATION OF MUSIC

In accordance with the company philosophy, the slogan of the brand DALI is, "In admiration of music." The goal of the company is to develop Hi-Fi loudspeakers for the stereo, home theater, and smart homes with an optimal sound reproduction. The company name, DALI, is an abbreviation for "Danish Audiophile Loudspeaker Industries." The design of the loudspeaker systems is aligned with typical Scandinavian design: functional shapes with clear-cut lines, natural color combinations and a harmonious mix of materials.

During product development, in-depth knowledge on the subject of audio technology and innovation production methods complement each other. Additionally, the subject of sustainability plays an increasingly important role at DALI. All of these factors combined have led to the success of the traditional Danish company. Their high-quality Hi-Fi products have already received numerous awards from prestigious competitions, such as the EISA Award from the Expert Imaging and Sound Association. DALI has also emerged as a supporter of musicians, enabling them to produce recordings at a high level of sound quality.

As the house brand of a Scandinavian Hi-Fi supplier, DALI was founded by Peter Lyngdorf in 1983 in Nørager, a small town in Northern Jutland. The Hi-Fi enthusiast still remains an influential person in the Danish audio industry today. Lars Worre has been advancing the company's development for more than 20 years. DALI has made an outstanding name for itself among quali-

ty-conscious sound lovers all over the world and holds multiple patents related to magnetic drives. Bucking the trend to outsource to low-wage countries, DALI produces its loudspeaker systems primarily in Denmark. Additional branches are located in Germany, Great Britain, the Benelux countries as well as in the Asia-Pacific region.

A major push for innovation has taken place over the past 10 years. Production processes have been rethought and adapted to the Danish location with modified procedures and materials, and made profitable despite a high wage structure. This method has created flexibility, an improved product quality and an obvious competitive advantage. DALI has been successful in evolving from a house brand to a loudspeaker manufacturer whose portfolio covers the entire spectrum, from starter products to luxury Hi-Fi systems, and they did it by developing groundbreaking products for the end user and doing continuous brand development in the premium segment. This was made possible by the staff's shared enthusiasm for musical sound experiences, which can be felt in the company's daily work.

With their luxury standing speaker "KORE," DALI reached a new milestone in the areas of sound quality and design in 2022. The high-end product is the flagship of decades of technology and product development and is based on the different loudspeaker series from the Danish manufacturer.

Factor

COMMUNICATION

Success has many factors. The strategic brand agency, Factor, views every single one of them from the perspective of what it does and what it's good for. Disrupting factors are eliminated, success factors are analyzed, and everything is optimally designed, down to the smallest details. Factor describes its métier as "factorizing brands."

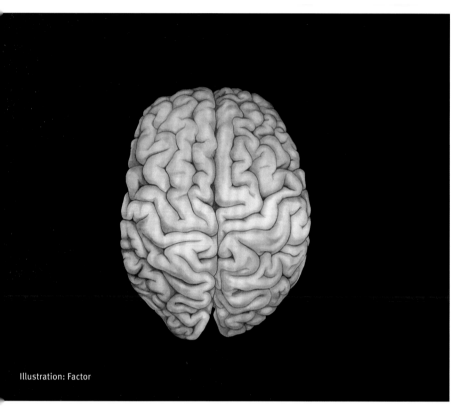

Illustration: Factor

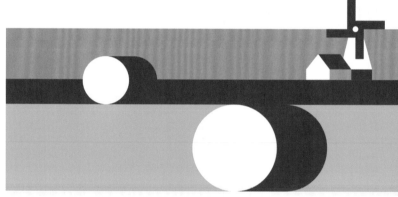

Illustration: Sonja Stroth (Factor)

3D-Artist: David Glissmann

Credit: Thomas Steuer

Factor Design was founded in May 1993 in Hamburg. The name of the company for communication design was Factor from the very beginning. Today, 30 years later, Factor is a successful company for the strategic alignment and differentiation of brands with their multi-faceted service portfolio: strategy, branding, digital, campaigning, and packaging. The customers come from different fields: seating furniture manufacturers, glass fiber providers, or banking institutes. Every brand is analyzed and repositioned using the Brand-Factorizer-Method developed by Factor itself.

While keeping the strengths, potential, and customers of a brand in mind, Factor develops brand positioning on the basis of the method, "Brand Activation Map," in order to optimize the success of a company on the market.

It is important to find the right communication strategy to convey the most compelling information in the most appropriate form. Factor will find the communication channels and media as well as the branding for an optimum effect and then develop product packaging for retail stores and digital shelves.

That is how the rebranding for a German glass fiber provider in a rural area was undertaken; how the design and communication of a Tyrol-based traditional producer of meat and sausage products were overhauled; and how the brand design, including packaging, for a manufacturer of sexual wellness products was completely redeveloped.

Ideally, clients would be supported by Factor over many years, because markets and customer expectations can change quickly in this fast-paced age.

In addition to the challenges of the market, the climate goals of the Climate Protection Program 2030 are dominating the futures of many companies. With Factor, you have an experienced partner on your side: "Large parts of products, their development, and production need to be completely reconsidered — business models will (need to) change. A radical rethink is necessary. Goals that were followed for many years — always faster, always higher, always further — will lose their meaning. We are supporting the upcoming change processes of our clients — we haven't really been doing anything else for the last 30 years — and will give a new identity to what is newly created."

One of Factor's special strengths is that it considers the final outcome and therefore achieves the best results in terms of content and visuals. Close collaboration with the clients, lots of creativity, and three decades of experience have built a strong foundation for further decades of successful brand strategies.

FACTS AND FIGURES

PRODUCTS
strategy, branding, digital, campaigning, packaging

LOCATIONS
Hamburg, Innsbruck, Vienna

FOUNDER
Olaf Stein (1993)

OWNERS
Mario Eckmaier, Axel Prey, Mareike Niggemann, Jörg Schweigert, Daniel Sorge, and Olaf Stein

EMPLOYEES
35+

SALES
DACH region, Europe

WEBSITE
factor.partners.com

FACTOR

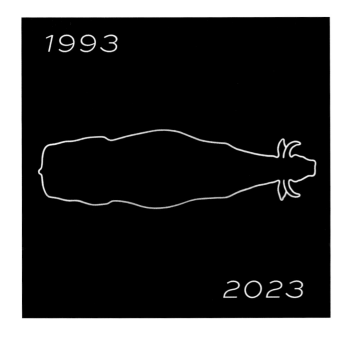

Credit: Rudi Schmutz Jr.

Dräger

MEDICAL AND SAFETY
TECHNOLOGY

Dräger counts among the leading international companies for medical and safety technology. The fifth-generation, family-owned company from Lübeck supports lifesavers worldwide in their work and protects breathing, whether during surgery, in the intensive care unit, during fire department operations, or during daily work in the industry.

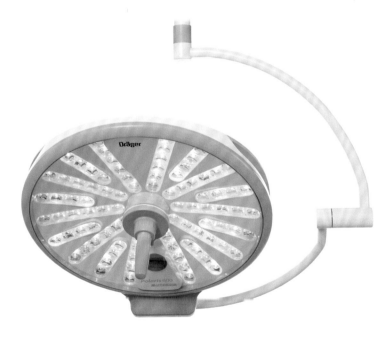

The multi-faceted range of products covers multiple areas of medical and safety technology. In the hospital, for example, Dräger products include patient data management systems, medical lights, and incubators are used in addition to anesthesia equipment and ventilators. Dräger provides customers from the hospital and mining industries with respiratory protection, protective clothing, and gas detection technology, among other things; they also provide firemen with especially ergonomic breathing apparatuses, as well as helmets, chemical protection suits and much more.

For more than 130 years, Dräger has represented values like trust, safety, and reliability, which give the company a high level of resilience. At first, when Johann Heinrich Dräger founded his company in 1889 in Lübeck, the company produced and sold the "Lubeca Valve," a pressure reducing valve for beer tap systems. In 1902, the first anesthesia mixing apparatus, the "Roth-Dräger," was brought out onto the market; in 1904, they developed the first reliable long-term mining apparatus, the "BG 1094;" and in 1907 came the first mass produced emergency ventilator, the "Pulmotor." The birth of the mobile gas measuring device was also groundbreaking in 1937: the so-called Dräger-Röhrchen measured contaminants and gasses in the surrounding air, in liquids, and in the ground.

The fundamentals of the corporate design have existed since 1983. The guiding principle, "Technology for life," has become even more apparent in the company's new appearance: the design breathes life. This is visible and tangible across all contact points, from product design to communication. "Life means constant change, and for the design as well, this means to maintain and develop, to change and reinvent, and to still remain who we are."

In an increasingly complex world, Dräger wants to remain clear, simple, and flexible, and ensure greater brand recognition with just a few unifying elements: One Dräger – One Design. The dark blue color stands for their traditional values, the light blue conveys awakening, the future, innovation strength, and the necessary freshness for breathing. Generous white areas convey the essential calm, which is reinforced by a superimposed font for all applications and gives the brand necessary clarity. An authentic visual language and the extensive use of user photos give their presence emotion.

"Technology for life," is more than a guiding principle for Dräger. Trust in Dräger products as well as the entire company as a business partner is regarded as a major responsibility that is met with proven quality, profound knowledge, pioneering innovations, and remaining creatively open to new ideas.

FACTS AND FIGURES

PRODUCTS
anesthesia devices and ventilators, gas measuring technology, respiratory protection

LOCATIONS
headquarters in Lübeck, production facilities in Germany, Chile, China, Great Britain, India, Sweden, South Africa, Czech Republic, USA, Norway, Switzerland

FOUNDER
Johann Heinrich Dräger
(1889, Lübeck)

OWNERS
the Dräger family

EMPLOYEES
15,900 worldwide (2021)

SALES
worldwide, own-brand sales and service companies in approx. 50 countries

WEBSITE
draeger.com

TIME TO BREATHE.

Dräger

The light blue elements are the visual trademark of all Dräger products.

Technik für das Leben

Technology for Life

RAL Farben

INTERNATIONALLY VALID COLOR STANDARDS

With its color scheme tools, systems, and services, RAL
Farben from Bonn sets internationally valid standards for
more than 2,500 tones of color. Professional designers
from all disciplines use them every day.

Credits: Prof. Timo Rieke

FACTS
AND FIGURES

PRODUCTS
internationally valid color standards,
supplementary services

LOCATIONS
Bonn,
Peking (since 2014)

FOUNDER
Reichskuratorium für Wirtschaftlichkeit
zur Vereinheitlichung technischer
Lieferbedingungen (1925, Berlin)

OWNER
RAL gGmbH

EMPLOYEES
70 (2022)

SALES
in more than 150 countries worldwide, more
than 40 distribution points, and online

WEBSITE
ral.de

How can you clearly explain which color a product should be printed or a website designed in? That is not a problem with the RAL color standards. Every color tone has a number that is internationally valid and has a descriptive name. The brand RAL Farben has stood for proven color communication for almost 100 years and delivers binding regulations for 2,540 color tones currently through its three-color palettes. The service encompasses products that range from supporting professional designers, to a color standardization that eases communication worldwide, to a transfer of knowledge via the "RAL Academy."

Most of the color standards are defined by the finely graduated "RAL DESIGN SYSTEM plus," with its 1,825 color tones; the color collection "RAL CLASSIC" encompasses 216 timeless colors; the high-end collection "RAL EFFECT" contains 70 metallic variations as well as 420 uniform color tones. In addition, the 300 most important colors from the RAL CLASSIC and RAL DESIGN SYSTEM plus collections are available as binding color samples for plastics.

Users of the color palettes primarily come from the fields of architecture and interior design, color consulting, artisans, universities, product design and industrial design. RAL Farben is part of the RAL gGmbH, which functions as a subsidiary of the RAL Deutsches Institut für Gütesicherung und Kennzeichnung. Since the mid 1920s, RAL has set the standard as experts for color.

In order to create uniform conditions for business, the company was founded in 1925 in Berlin as the "Reichsausschuss for Lieferbedingungen," (RAL, Imperial Committee for Delivery Conditions). Among other reasons, this was in order to respond to changes in the industrial manufacturing processes, such as the emergence of assembly line production. In 1927 the first color tones were standardized and normalized in the "RAL 840-HR" color registry. At this point in time, the collection contained 40 different tones.

Today, the "RAL K7" is the most sold color fan internationally. It contains all 216 tones of the historically evolved color collection RAL CLASSIC, but provides for a quick overview through its

compact design. Since 2020, the color orange with the number 2017 has defined the house color of the color experts.

The leaders of the company regularly ask themselves how they can improve their offering of products and services, in order to support creativity in the best possible way. At the same time, unstable global conditions have generated new challenges. Set against the background of current developments, innovative solutions are becoming increasingly important for long-term success.

The search for sustainable and resource-saving solutions plays a fundamental role at RAL Farben. In order to continue to be a strong partner in the future, the company deploys new production technologies and uses alternative raw materials. Products and their transformations are continually developed further in order to develop innovative application ranges. This is also why RAL won their fourth German Design Award in 2020, this time for the design box "RAL Starter-Kit" which provided quick access to the "RAL DESIGN SYSTEM plus".

Wöhner

ELECTRICAL TECHNOLOGY

The Wöhner success story begins with the development of their first products at home on the kitchen table. In 1929 Alfred Wöhner founded his company, today an internationally renowned specialist in the fields of energy distribution, control technology, and renewable energies.

The groundbreaking product innovation at the time was a new type of three-pole fuse socket for Siemens, which was both space-saving and particularly easy to install. Today, Wöhner stands for more than 90 years of innovation.

Loyal to their motto "Alles mit Spannung" (everything with voltage), Wöhner stands for future-oriented technologies for the distribution and control of electrical energy. With their high level of innovative ability, paired with passion and creative freedom, the company has been successful in taking on a pioneering role.

An outstanding Wöhner product is the 60 mm busbar system: developed in-house, established as the standard in the field of low-voltage distribution and control technology, and today the most used busbar system in many branches for varied industrial use.

In the product category of "busbar system technology," Wöhner was honored in 2022 as Brand of the Century for successfully defining an entire genre of products or services and setting the standard in its field. Further highlights in their portfolio include the touch-safe protected power distribution system, Crossboard, the busbar system 185Power as well as their latest groundbreaking innovation: the MOTUS C14, a fuseless, resettable electronic motor protector that reacts faster than any fuse. In the event of a fault, the innovative C14 technology makes it possible to shut the motor down within a maximum of 10 microseconds.

Wöhner doesn't only set the standard with numerous technical solutions, but also places a strong emphasis on quality and design. High-quality materials guarantee proven durability and stability and value retention; the blue viewing window and the consciously amorphous form provide for a high level of brand recognition. The uniqueness and quality of the brand as an important factor of success is highly valued internally as well, as it conveys pride and direction and strengthens the level of passion.

Thanks to a slim structure and its own complete process chain, Wöhner can react to changes quickly, adapt flexibly, and bring new projects to market maturity in a relatively short amount of time. In order to tap into other industries and markets, Wöhner also now manufactures electronic components in addition to electromechanical components. Looking to the future as a specialist in energy issues, Wöhner is focusing on the energy revolution and climate protection. Wöhner also takes responsibility for future generations. Today, Wöhner is already climate neutral and is implementing a variety of measures to reduce CO_2 emissions. In addition to optimizing their energy needs, their use of resources has been steadily minimized thanks to the use of regenerative energy for internal consumption. Reduced use of plastics and the first bio-based materials made from renewable, plant-based resources also reduce their CO_2 footprint. Wöhner's goal is to become climate positive in the coming years, and also to deliver an important push toward a climate-friendly energy supply at the societal level through the control and efficient distribution of electrical energy.

FACTS AND FIGURES

OWNERS
the Frank Wöhner family

FOUNDER
Alfred Wöhner (1929, Rödental)

PRODUCTS
from electromechanical products to safety and busbar systems, to intelligent energy distribution, electronic components, and software services

LOCATIONS
Rödental (headquarters); 12 subsidiaries abroad, production locations in Rödental (Germany), Hampton (USA), Peking (China), Boituva (Brazil)

SALES
in more than 80 countries worldwide

EMPLOYEES
390 employees worldwide, 230 of them at the Rödental location

WEBSITE
woehner.de

wöhner
ALLES MIT SPANNUNG

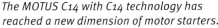
The MOTUS C14 with C14 technology has reached a new dimension of motor starters.

The CrossBoard creates organization and space in the control cabinet.

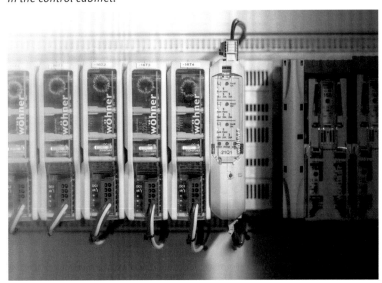

sonoro audio

GERMAN AUDIO AND DESIGN

sonoro combines brilliant sound in the high-fidelity segment with award-winning design, high-quality workmanship and optimal user-friendliness.

GERMAN AUDIO
AND DESIGN

Music is one of the greatest passions of humanity. Listening to music is one of the most popular free time activities across all age groups. Although the younger generation uses omnipresent mobile devices in order to listen to the latest chart hits anytime and anywhere, the classic hi-fi stereo system has successfully survived over decades. Today's customers are placing greater emphasis on quality. Flawless, pure sound in a wide range of room conditions is as important as contemporary design. sonoro audio systems fit perfectly into any interior design with their design and color customized by the user, and become part of the room or stand out as an eyecatcher.

Since 2006, Marcell Faller, founder and CEO of sonoro audio GmbH from Neuss, has focused with his forty person team on letting their own enthusiasm for music contribute to the development of unique music systems.

sonoro concentrates its technical efforts on the development of music systems that impress with their sound. For sonoro, the sound quality factor is inseparably connected to the characteristics of the room that contains the audio system. To put it simply, sonoro understands that a bathroom sounds different than a living room or a kitchen does, which is why they offer the perfect sound source for every room and every everyday situation. With compact all-in-one devices, high-fidelity loudspeakers developed in-house, and hi-fi receivers, sonoro has made a name for itself as a brand among music lovers in recent years. The most popular models MEISTERSTÜCK and MAESTRO are compelling thanks to not only their functionality, user-friendliness and contemporary compatibility with different audio sources, but also through their timeless modern design.

The brand owes numerous awards to this combination of form and function. Outstanding achievements in the area of product design have been confirmed by the Red Dot Design Award 2020, for example. The prestigious design competition honored the two bestsellers MAESTRO and MEISTERSTÜCK and recognized their developer's top performance in aesthetics, material composition, craftsmanship, surface structure, ergonomics, and functionality.

As a brand, sonoro also convinced the expert jury of the Plus X Award®, as well as the German Brand Award 2021. They were recognized not only for design and brand management, but also for the technical performance of sonoro products. At the Fidelity Award 2020, the MEISTERSTÜCK was once again among the winners of the "Premium Award" in the category "Streaming Radio."

According to sonoro, all the awards and the success of the brand among its customers are the result of a compelling performance by its team of audio and design experts and their strong identification with the sonoro brand.

FACTS AND FIGURES

PRODUCTS
designer audio systems

LOCATION
Neuss

FOUNDER
Marcell Faller (2006)

OWNER
Marcell Faller

EMPLOYEES
40 (2022)

SALES
DACH region as well as select markets in Europe and internationally, via specialty stores and online

WEBSITE
sonoro.com

The bestseller MEISTERSTÜCK offers all-in-one music enjoyment. The turntable PLATINUM SE pays homage to the vinyl revival.

Every transformative process happens in the area of tension between revolution and evolution.

PROF. MIKE RICHTER

Jung von Matt
BRAND
IDENTITY

COMMUNICATION, CONSULTING

As a specialist agency for identity and brand development, Jung von Matt BRAND IDENTITY helps companies to reach their full potential and create comprehensive, consistent brand experiences. The service provider itself is a part of an internationally successful brand agency.

There are lots of companies; whether or not they will become a brand is ultimately decided by the customer alone. What they associate with a name, a logo, or a specific design is what distinguishes a brand. This perception differentiates goods and services from otherwise largely identical competitors and significantly influences the purchase decision.

The creation of brands is seldom a product of coincidence. An intensive amount of work is behind the leading brands in every conceivable industry. Brands are precisely developed, established, and managed long-term. Jung von Matt BRAND IDENTITY supports companies during the analysis, strategy, and development of brands. Their stated goal is to establish brands as lived identities that achieve identification, enthusiasm, credibility, and trust.

As an independent branding agency, Jung von Matt BRAND IDENTITY is part of the Jung von Matt family and also uses that expertise to rethink and further develop brands on behalf of the customer. At the same time, it is necessary to make the brands future-proof and to support them in their transformation to the network age, in order to improve their market performance and strengthen it sustainably for the competition.

Under the motto, "We love ideas that inspire," Jung von Matt BRAND IDENTITY perceives brands as the sum of all the characteristics of an identity that provide advantages. The agency orients itself on the defined cornerstones of strong internal and external brand experiences: clarity, consistency, continuity, credibility, and commitment. With this comprehensive understanding, they develop sound strategies as prerequisites for the momentum and success of a brand.

As one of a total of eight Jung von Matt agencies from Jung von Matt Switzerland, the core competencies of Jung von Matt BRAND IDENTITY are brand strategy, brand personality, brand trans-

model-group.com

MODEL

See the Extra in the Ordinary

formation, brand ecosystems, brand design, and brand management. At the same time, Jung von Matt's well-known visual identity, which has been successful for many years, is used to represent the company's own brand.

Since its founding in August of 2011, numerous successful brands have been counted among the clients that have built on the expertise of Jung von Matt BRAND IDENTITY over the course of their development. From the transformation of the ZF Friedrichshafen AG to Next Generation Mobility, to the new identity of the Model Group, to the comprehensive strategic and visual brand consulting for the Swiss Post; Jung von Matt BRAND IDENTITY is behind the success of a constantly growing number of national and international brands.

FACTS AND FIGURES

PRODUCTS
services such as brand strategy, brand development, and brand management

LOCATIONS
Zurich: Jung von Matt
BRAND IDENTITY
Europe, Asia, USA: Jung von Matt

FOUNDER
Prof. Dr. Dominique von Matt

MANAGING DIRECTOR
Dr. Thomas Deigendesch

EMPLOYEES
15 (JvM BRAND IDENTITY),
140 (JvM Switzerland),
1,500 (JvM total)

WEBSITE
jvmbrandidentity.ch

JUNGvMATT
BRAND IDENTITY

Tilia

CHAIRS, ARMCHAIRS, AND TABLES
MADE OF PLASTIC FOR OUTDOOR
AREAS AND BUSINESSES

The plastic furniture made by the Turkish brand Tilia is appealingly designed, sustainable, and affordable for all. Thanks to this, the company based in Istanbul has won numerous prestigious design awards.

The brand Tilia emerged from the company Savaş Plastic, which was founded in 1963 by Sadettin Savaş in Istanbul. Initially, it specialized in the production of shirt buttons and combs made of plastic. With the know-how and the experience of their longtime employees, the company began to produce plastic furniture under the brand name Tilia in 1999. The founders of Tilia are Ali Savaş and Mustafa Savaş, the second generation of the family-owned company.

The armchair Atra, created by designer Kunter Şekercioğlu clearly reflects their principle of democratic design, according to which furniture from Tilia is created: they are well designed, durable, and affordable for all. The seat surface of the stackable plastic armchair, which is equally as suitable for use in interior rooms as well as outdoor areas, can be removed, changed, and recycled. Atra is weatherproof and easy to clean. The decorative hole pattern of the seating furniture creates natural ventilation. These features have brought the product of the Turkish manufacturer numerous prestigious design awards, including the German Design Award 2021 in Gold.

With more than half a century of experience and the strong belief in innovation, the company constantly improves itself and its production processes. Its team of experts develop and produce long-lasting products of high quality, that are user-friendly and offer practical solutions for daily life. The certified plastic furniture consists of materials that are weatherproof and easy to clean. Polypropylene is primarily used for production, which is made even more stable and

durable through the additional use of fiberglass in some designs. These materials are 100 percent recyclable and can be produced without waste.

Tilia values recycling as a contemporary possibility to create new products. That is why the manufacturer produces its chairs, armchairs, and tables from completely recyclable materials. Even by-products and waste products are added back into the production cycle, in order to produce long-lasting furniture that makes the customers happy. Currently, Tilia delivers its sustainable plastic furniture to more than 60 countries.

FACTS AND FIGURES

PRODUCTS
chairs, armchairs, and tables made from plastic for outdoor areas and businesses

LOCATION
Istanbul

FOUNDER
Sadettin Savaş (1963, Istanbul)

OWNERS
family-owned company in its third generation

SALES
Europe, Middle East, North America

WEBSITE
tilia.info

HEY-SIGN

INTERIOR DESIGN SECTOR

When searching for sustainable and environmentally friendly materials, many manufacturers depend on innovative new developments. HEY-SIGN uses its view into the past and transports traditional wool felt into the future.

Archeological discoveries from the Bronze Age have proven that felt is very probably the oldest textile in the history of mankind. However, the material and its production techniques have been largely forgotten over the recent decades. Clothing made of wool felt is no more than a niche product today. For more than 20 years, HEY-SIGN has been working successfully on a comeback for the traditional material and presents unique products for the interior design sector, which are compelling, not only for their visual appearance, but especially due to the characteristic features of the material.

The natural material, made from the renewable raw material new wool, is breathable, abrasion-resistant, stable in form, low-maintenance, durable, and skin-friendly. At the same time, it possesses insulating and sound-absorption features, and can be used specifically to improve the room climate and acoustics.

As a specialist and pioneer in wool felt processing, HEY-SIGN produces living accessories such as pillows, baskets, and table decorations, as well as chair and bench cushions, seating, rugs, and many more decorative elements and utensils for use in private homes, offices, and commercial spaces. In addition, acoustic elements, curtains, and room partitions in bespoke measurements offer optimal conditions for a visually appealing, climatic, and acoustic interior design.

The timeless, multi-award-winning design in combination with fresh colors, constitutes the central element of HEY-SIGN creations. That is how the transformation of traditional materials to a foundation of contemporary furnishings has been successful. HEY-SIGN has paved the way for wool felt to enter the world of living and working and has proven once again, after spending decades on the back burner, that it is suitable as a sustainable and functional lifestyle product.

The wool felt that HEY-SIGN works with is naturally sustainable. The mulesing-free wool felt consists of 100 percent pure new wool, carries the quality seal from "The Woolmark Company," and is certified to Oeko-Tex® standard 100. The production of HEY-SIGN products is done by hand and "Made in Germany." Parts of the collection are produced at workshops for adapted work and at local suppliers for metal, wood and leather. HEY-SIGN also insists on short transport distances.

In order to strengthen the HEY-SIGN brand and lead it successfully into the future, the founders, Bernadette Ehmanns and Matthias Hey, decided to partner with the BWF Group in 2019, the leading manufacturer of designer felt for lifestyle and interiors as well as innovation partners with international presence. Since then, HEY-SIGN, under the management of its longtime employee Katharina Günther, has been part of this traditional company, which in turn can look back on a 126-year history in wool felt production.

FACTS AND FIGURES

PRODUCTS
furnishings, furniture, and accessories made of wool felt in four thicknesses and more than 40 color tones

LOCATION
Meerbusch, North Rhein Westphalia

FOUNDER
Bernadette Ehmanns and Matthias Hey (1999, Meerbusch)

OWNERS
HEY-SIGN is a company belonging to the BWF Group.

EMPLOYEES
32

SALES
specialist stores, online stores, and HEY-SIGN online shop

WEBSITE
hey-sign.de

INNOVATION IN FELT

Bette

PLUMBING

The medium-sized, third generation family-operated company, which was founded in 1952 by Heinrich Bette in Delbrück, is a specialist for bathroom elements made of glazed titanium steel. The forming technique, which was developed by engineer Fritz-Wilhelm Pahl himself, is the foundation for their success.

Courage and an inventive spirit pay-off: the history of the Bette company is a good example. When there was no money to pay for an off-the-peg system in the 1970s, the young engineer, father of the current managing director, designed his own machine concept, which is still the foundation for revolutionary innovations today. During the unique forming technique, the steel is not stretched but poured into the mold during the deep-drawing process, making it highly precise and stable. Basic forms can then be customized. There is a choice of 400 different colors and numerous additional features can be added. Exclusive special editions are manufactured by hand. Apropos manufacturing: despite the size of the company, all products are still manufactured exclusively in East Westphalia today.

Examples of revolutionary developments by Bette are the first free-standing, seamless bath; the first floor-level shower area, BetteFloor; as well as the first shower tile, BetteAir, which can be installed directly on the floor, like a tile, thanks to a new style of installation, and where the drainage design is one-of-a-kind.

The design is architecture related and characterized by technical finesse as well as aesthetics. In close collaboration with renowned designers, the limits of steel forming are continually redefined, because the greatest passion at Bette is the, "intelligent connection between product and building envelope."

The bathroom elements made of long-lasting glazed titanium steel are extremely light due to the especially thin material, and still extraordinarily robust; its brilliant surface made from BetteGlasur® is harder than marble, plastic, and steel, and is scratchproof, nonporous, and UV resistant. Bette offers a 30-year guarantee for its premium quality. The long-life of the bathroom elements also contributes to a good eco-balance.

The materials steel and glass present many industrial companies with the challenge of developing a production that is as low in CO_2 as possible. Since Bette has always been committed to the careful use of natural resources, the company already uses green steel, and intends to increase the proportion that it uses even further. They have invested extensively in energy generation as well. For so-called circular products, recycled materials are incorporated, and the company's fuel-saving trucks always drive with fully loaded cargo areas; even on their return routes, for which they cooperate with other companies logistically. Bette views sustainability as an ongoing commitment because, "sustainability is our mission — and not just a fashionable buzzword."

FACTS AND FIGURES

PRODUCTS
bathroom elements made of glazed titanium steel (bathtubs, showers, washbasins) and accessories for a secure connection to the building envelope

LOCATION
Delbrück (headquarters) in East Westphalia; Great Britain, China, Russia

FOUNDER
Heinrich Bette
(1952, Delbrück)

OWNERS
the Pahl family

EMPLOYEES
395 (2022)

SALES
worldwide

WEBSITE
my-bette.com

BETTE

THE BEST
FOR THE BATH

PROLED

HIGH QUALITY LED LIGHTING

The brand PROLED is a pioneer of LED technology. For more than 20 years, the innovative German company has delivered exemplary lighting solutions for interior rooms and outdoor areas.

PROLED Flex Strip Opal Shape

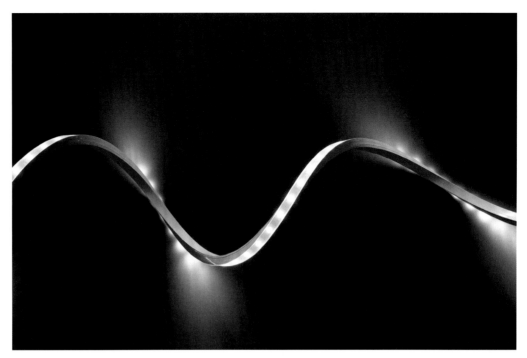

Left: PROLED Flex Line Porter. Right: PROLED Flex Strip Wall.

At PROLED, high quality light and good lighting are paramount. The LED products of the company, located in the Bavarian city of Friedberg, make precise linear as well as architecturally technical lighting with spots and downlights possible. Versatile solutions for the outdoors round out their portfolio. PROLED views itself as a pioneer in LED technology and is a leading supplier on the LED market, so innovation is part of their daily business. As a part of the PROLED Group, the organization is also a strong player on the international level. As a manufacturer with in-house divisions for design, engineering, and testing, the lighting experts stand for high quality, sustainable, and affordable products.

The company was founded under the name MBN in 1988 by Bernd Menrad, who continued to lead the company until 2021. In 2005, he established the house brand PROLED, at which point he began to manufacture LED lighting exclusively. In 2021, CEO Peter Gawlik took over the management of the design and system lighting manufacturer mawa, as well as the firm MBN with his brand PROLED. Both companies, as well as the company UNIBRIGHT, belong to the PROLED GROUP.

The current focus is on the new products, "PROLED Flex Strip Opal Shape," and "PROLED Flex Strip Wall." Both have proven to be extremely flexible in their application and form with maximum lighting quality. With Shape, a wide variety of room atmospheres can be designed, thanks to its homogenous 360° emittance. Wall functions as an extremely precise and powerful wall illumination. The high-tech products are used by light planners, architects, and interior designers in order to create custom lighting solutions.

Having the highest quality standards for customizations, light measurements and IP testing are a matter of course for PROLED. That includes the customization of aluminum profiles and plastic covers in the length requested, Flex Strips with individual cable input as well as the assembly of functional "plug and play" units. With standardized leak tests, the suitability of all outdoor and underwater products for operation in certain environmental conditions is checked, and the correct IP rating can be guaranteed. Beyond that, exact photometric measurements are taken in the in-house laboratory. There, the faultless functioning of the luminaires and components is tested, from relevant quality parameters such as power consumption and luminous flux, spectrum, color temperature and color rendering, as well as flicker-free operation and glare.

In addition to the PROLED headquarters in Friedberg, the company also manages the subsidiary PROLED AUSTRIA as well as PROLED SWITZERLAND. There is also a particular focus on the Italian market.

FACTS AND FIGURES

PRODUCTS
high quality LED lighting

LOCATION
Friedberg, Bavaria

FOUNDER
Bernd Menrad (2005, Friedberg)

OWNER
PROLED GROUP

EMPLOYEES
60 (2022)

SALES
worldwide via sales representatives, branches and distributing agencies

WEBSITE
proled.com

Nowy Styl

COMPLETE FURNISHINGS FOR OFFICES AND PUBLIC SPACES

Nowy Styl's goal is to make working more efficient and more comfortable through customized solutions and holistic concepts. The company will celebrate its 30 year anniversary this year.

As one of the leading manufacturers in Europe, Nowy Styl offers complete furnishings for the arrangement of offices and public spaces such as airports, clinics, multipurpose halls, and cinemas. In 1992, brothers Adam and Jerzy Krzanowski founded their seating factory in Krosno, Poland, in order to produce their brand's first seating models. Just one year later they had more than 100 employees. In 2000, the company reached the milestone of having sold one million chairs. In addition, they continually expand their portfolio in order to reach new customers and market segments.

Today, the brand Kusch+Co also belongs to their business group, which is popular for its product designs as well as innovative solutions for passenger terminals and healthcare facilities. Their holistic concept has made their business unique. Nowy Styl creates custom rooms, from the planning to the manufacturing to the final product. Their modern solutions also include office concepts for hybrid working arrangements as well as furniture for flexible working and remote work. At the moment, the group is active in more than 100 countries. In 2022, they celebrated their 30 year anniversary and opened a new showroom in Berlin.

Nowy Styl, "New Style" in Polish, has designed the office spaces of international concerns such as Toyota, ABB, Siemens, and Deloitte, among others. In recent years, the company has invested in new manufacturing technologies. With a specialized software application, they are able to configure standard products according to the customer's requests and ideas. During the CO_2 reduced production, materials that are eco-friendly, recyclable or already recycled are used. Nowy Styl was recognized in 2022 with the EcoVadis Platinum Medallion, which honors the top one percent of audited companies for exemplary environmental performance and business ethics, as well as sustainable supply chains.

The product portfolio contains ergonomic chairs and tables, multi-functional furniture, soft seating solutions, furniture for the home office, acoustic panels, hospital facilities, as well as the furnishing of airport and harbor terminals, theaters and stadiums. Everything is based on the know-how and experience of a team of experts, which consists of engineers, technologists, architects, programmers, managers, and psychologists and sociologists, in addition to designers. In order to offer the highest quality, all products are continuously tested and checked for durability.

Among the brand's award-winning products is the office chair "V-Care" from Justus Kolberg for Kusch+Co, which won the Red Dot Design Award in 2022. In addition, the swivel chair "WithME" from Nowy Styl (Design: Martin Ballendat) received the German Innovation Award in 2021. The modular series "Creva Desk" and "Creva Soft" seating were winners of the Iconic Award 2021 and the German Design Award 2021. Both programs developed the Cologne design office Kaschkasch for Kusch+Co. Renowned product designers such as these will continue to make a decisive contribution to Nowy Styl's success in the future.

FACTS AND FIGURES

PRODUCTS
holistic furnishings for offices and public spaces

LOCATIONS
Krosno, Berlin, Düsseldorf, Steyerberg, Ebermannsdorf; more than 30 showrooms worldwide

FOUNDERS
Adam and Jerzy Krzanowski
(1992, Krosno)

BOARD MEMBERS
Adam and Jerzy Krzanowski,
Rafał Chwast,
Roman Przybylski

EMPLOYEES
more than 5,900 including all joint ventures (2021)

SALES
in 18 countries in Europe and the Near East

WEBSITE
nowystyl.com

NowyStyl

In response to constantly changing requirements, including in the office, Nowy Styl offers customized and functional furnishing solutions that enable flexible working.

KLUDI

METAL INDUSTRY / SANITARY INDUSTRY

The company, founded in 1926 in Sauerland, stands for almost 100 years of experience in the development and production of high-quality fittings for bathrooms and kitchens. The manufacturer of times-gone-by has long since become a globally recognized fittings specialist and a modern industrial company.

The fittings specialist unites functionality, innovation, and design in products of first-class quality. With groundbreaking solutions, KLUDI has proven again and again that it is a trendsetter. For example, KLUDI replaced the cumbersome pull up diverters on single-lever concealed faucets for the bathtub with an innovative valve solution: a comfortable push-button solution (KLUDI PUSH & SWITCH) and with it, set a new standard. Real value for the user is offered through more developments from this medium-sized company, such as the first hybrid fitting worldwide for the kitchen sink (KLUDI E-GO); the flexible aerator (KLUDI s-pointer), which allows the spray angle to be adjusted to optimally fit the sink; the bayonet connection, for the under-window installation of kitchen fittings; and the KLUDI multi-connector, an integrated shut-off valve for the washing machine and dishwasher. Their strength in innovation and wealth of ideas are reflected in the approximately 170 inventions and more than 100 patents that they hold. This innovation strength contributes significantly to their competitive ability and future viability. This is not only about products, but also a fundamental willingness to question the established and rethink the familiar. So KLUDI now avoids using plastic in its packaging and uses recyclable and biodegradable materials instead.

From casting brass to the final installation, KLUDI is one of the few manufacturers in Germany that possesses its own comprehensive fittings production. In addition, the company also develops and constructs all necessary production tools itself.

Because KLUDI manufactures products that people touch and use countless times every day, the company attaches great importance to good design. For KLUDI, that is not only about the form and aesthetics, but also functionality, ease of use, and emotions. KLUDI considers a design successful when it serves people and creates a tangible added value.

KLUDI lives the partnership with its professional customers, going far beyond just business. The KLUDI future workshop offers a platform for interaction between tradesman companies and KLUDI management, on eye-level, from medium-sized company to medium-sized company to ask where the proverbial shoe pinches the skilled trade. The intention behind this is to jointly develop solutions to urgent challenges and make life a little easier for their market partners in the face of a complex environment.

FACTS AND FIGURES

PRODUCTS
fittings for the bathroom and kitchen

LOCATIONS
Menden (headquarters and central office), Production locations:
Menden (Germany),
Hornstein (Austria),
Diösd (Hungary),

FOUNDER
Franz Scheffer (1926, Menden)

OWNERS
RAK Ceramics Group,
Ras Al Khaimah/Vereinigte Arabische Emirate (since 2022)

EMPLOYEES
more than 860 total,
more than 350 in Germany

SALES
in more than 100 countries in Europe, Asia, Africa, America, Oceania via KLUDI sales branches or importers

WEBSITE
kludi.com

WATER IN PERFECTION

KLUDI
WATER IN PERFECTION

The archetype of the new zeitgeist: KLUDI NOVA FONTE Pura captivates with its unique, delicate design.

Ca Go Bike

BICYCLE INDUSTRY

The mobility revolution and energy turnaround can only succeed with innovative mobility concepts. Ca Go Bike has transformed the classic cargo bike into a modern means of transport with the highest safety standards.

The combination of bicycle and load carrier belongs to the urban landscape in cities in particular. Delivery services and couriers value the car alternative thanks to its flexibility and inexpensive maintenance costs. As a lifestyle product, it serves to promote the next generation and is a statement for a sustainable lifestyle.

With the economically and ecologically necessary mobility revolution, the interest in cargo bicycles is growing parallel to classic bicycles as a versatile alternative in cargo and passenger transport. At the same time, growing demand in electric bicycles also opens up new applications for cargo bicycles.

With a focus on the aspects of safety, usability, and design, the brand Ca Go has dedicated itself to the further development of modern urban micro mobility in the form of the electric cargo bicycle since 2018. The company was originally founded with the aim of marketing the transport box developed by company founders Franc Arnold and Thorsten Michel, which was designed as a passenger compartment. When this didn't succeed right away, the duo decided to establish and develop their own e-cargo bicycle. In 2019, Ca Go presented its first model, the FS200 Life, which was followed three years later by the new model FS200 Vario in 2022.

From the beginning, the focus of development has been on children's safety, and the specially constructed passenger compartment has been designed to transport them. The EPP-CargoBox from the Ca Go FS200 Life is made from shock-absorbing expanded polypropylene and can be equipped with ergonomic child seats that have a five-point safety belt, as well as height-adjustable headrests and an optional safety collar. To sum up: independent crash tests have confirmed that the Ca Go FS200 Life has a successful safety concept and a low risk of injury.

Ca Go conforms to the highest quality standards in the technology and design of both its models. Beginning with the powerful Bosch Performance CX Cargo Line Motor, the enviolo AUTOMATIQ transmission, the Magura disc brakes, and the SUPERNOVA light system, the Ca Go FS200 offers everything necessary for a safe, long-lasting, and easy operation.

Although the safety aspect is at the center of development for the Ca Go team, consisting of high-level experts in the bicycle and automobile industries, Ca Go is also compelling when it comes to product design. This has been confirmed by the numerous awards that the young company has received since its founding- in particular the Focus E-Bike Design & Innovation Award 2019, the German Design Award 2021 and the Red Dot Design Award 2022. Ca Go is especially impressive as an innovative new development in the field of e-mobility, which was underscored by the German Innovation Award 2021 in the e-mobility category.

FACTS AND FIGURES

PRODUCTS
innovative e-cargo bicycles according to the highest equipment and safety standards

LOCATION
Koblenz

FOUNDERS
Franc Arnold and Thorsten Michel (2018, Koblenz)

OWNERS
Franc Arnold and Thorsten Michel

EMPLOYEES
approx. 40 (2022)

SALES
Händler- und Partnervertrieb, DACH-Region

WEBSITE
cagobike.com

For all your precious cargo.

Das FS200 Vario Aktionsmodell „Open-Pro" und das FS200 Life Aktionsmodell „Family-Plus".

MÜHLE

HANDCRAFTED ACCESSORIES
FOR A CLEAN SHAVE

From their headquarters in the Erzgebirge region of Saxony, the brand Mühle has evolved into a leading international supplier of exclusive accessories for the wet shave.

Otto Johannes Müller created his first shaving brush with the brand name Mühle in a laundry room in 1945. The company headquarters has remained in the municipality of Stützengrün in the Erzgebirge region of Saxony since that time. High quality products related to shaving are still handcrafted there, now supported by modern technology. Brush-making is traditional to the region, which is why the employees have so much expertise and finesse when it comes to their craftsmanship. This is how Mühle was able to evolve itself into one of the leading international suppliers for high-quality accessories for the wet shave. But it was a long way to get there...

After the death of the founder, his son, Hans-Jürgen Müller took over his family's company in 1965. Seven years later, the company was affected by the wave of expropriation in the DDR- Müller was only able to gain it back with the reunification of Germany. In the following years he fought for economic survival, reorganized his company and was successful in establishing the brand. The third generation, brothers Andreas and Christian Müller, have led the company since 2008. In 2014, the Mühle store in Berlin was opened; a showroom in London followed four years later. Beyond that, the family is involved in the "Verein deutscher Manufakturen" (Association of German Manufacturers) for the appreciation and preservation of manufactory work.

Mühle brought the long-lasting "Silvertip Fibre" onto the market as an international innovation. These synthetically produced and low-maintenance fibers dry much faster than any natural material. They are especially soft at their ends, while a firmer lower brush section creates a comfortable massage effect. As with all Mühle products, they are produced by solid craftsmanship together with industrial precision, the finest materials, and a consistently sustainable approach.

At this point, the distinguished product portfolio contains many classics. It is complemented by new designs with a high aesthetic standard. That includes the "Hexagon" series by Mark Braun, which won the 2017 Red Dot Award. 2021 saw the launch of the first unisex safety razor: "Companion." As the current bestseller in the range, it makes a plastic-free shave of the body and face possible- a method that more and more women are coming to appreciate.

In advancing its portfolio, Mühle is inspired by external designers, trends, and cooperation partners such as the brands Herr von Eden or the porcelain manufacturer Meissen. At the center of the brand is the aspiration to create products of an outstanding design quality, which are sustainable in every respect — beginning with the resource-conserving production with green energy and regional supply chains, to CO_2 neutral shipping, to repairs and recycling. These values are the basis for the brand's actions and will continue to determine them in the future.

FACTS AND FIGURES

PRODUCTS
handcrafted accessories for
wet shaving

LOCATIONS
Stützengrün in the Erzgebirge region,
stores in Berlin and London

FOUNDER
Otto Johannes Müller
(1945, Stützengrün)

OWNER
family-owned company in the
third generation, Christian and
Andreas Müller

EMPLOYEES
75 (2022)

SALES
via distribution partners worldwide

WEBSITE
muehle-shaving.com

MÜHLE

Credit: Mirko Hertel

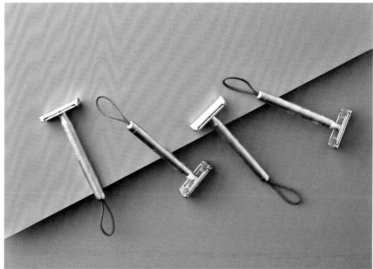

AXENT
Switzerland

SANITARY TECHNOLOGY

The bathroom combines functionality, individual taste and stylish zeitgeist more than any other room in the house. The Swiss company AXENT has especially distinguished itself in that regard: they combine innovative technology with one-of-a-kind design.

Since its founding in 2008, the AXENT Group has developed into a leading international manufacturer of sanitary technology. The product portfolio of the company from Rapperswil-Jona in the Swiss canton of St. Gallen encompasses innovative, cutting-edge technology for shower toilets, high quality sanitary ware, shower systems and bathroom fittings as well as innovative performance technology for bathroom products.

The founders had already emphasized their company philosophy through the name that they chose: the brand name AXENT is meant to be understood as a homophone to the adjective "excellent," and therefore an unmistakable statement about their quality standards.

AXENT combines comprehensive knowledge of their field with irrepressible curiosity about the future. Six hundred engineers in research and development are constantly looking at the bathroom from new perspectives and pushing the limits of what is possible. More than 3,200 employees share the AXENT Group's vision: to become the most innovative and reliable provider of sanitary technology in the world. Not least because of this, AXENT opened a subsidiary in the USA and a base in Switzerland for Europe and the Middle East; optimal conditions to strengthen customer relations and expand their global scope.

Together with designers Matteo Thun, Antonio Rodriguez, and Arthur Eisenkrein, AXENT believes in the principle of creating simplicity from complexity. Perfection is not achieved when there is nothing else to add, but rather when there is nothing left to take away. This is reflected especially in the award-winning shower toilet AXENT.Meta, which fits perfectly into every bathroom.

The new shower toilet is a result of innovative ideas, patented technologies and innovative details. Equipped with the latest AXENT.Infinity flush technology, the water consumption is significantly lower and the noise level much quieter than typical toilets. Thanks to the specialized hinge design, the seat and cover no longer need to be disassembled in order to clean the ceramic surface. The nozzle is stainless steel and sprays water that has been enriched with oxygen-rich bubbles for a gentle, refreshing, and skin-friendly shower sensation.

Due to the characteristic AXENT design, shaped by elegant curved lines and a harmonious surface, the boundaries between shower toiler and design object are blurred.

AXENT Switzerland has consistently won first-class international awards since 2012, and has convinced top clients, architects, and designers through its perfect combination of technology and design.

FACTS AND FIGURES

PRODUCTS
shower toilets, sanitary ware,
shower systems, bathroom fittings,
performance technology for
bathroom products.

LOCATIONS
Switzerland (base), USA, China

MANAGING DIRECTOR
Daniel Grob

EMPLOYEES
3,250 (2022)

SALES
Europe, Middle East, Asia and
America

WEBSITE
axentbath.eu

Can good design increase the crisis resistance of companies or even entire industries?

LUTZ DIETZOLD

Oventrop

BUILDING AND HOME TECHNOLOGY

Oventrop is the partner for efficient heating, cooling, and clean potable water. With the modular system and modular services from the family business, owner-operated since 1851, sanitation, heating and air conditioning service providers are able to work easily and flexibly, since they are able to combine pioneering solutions depending on the requirements.

The company was founded in 1851 by Arnold Oventrop as the "Arnold Oventrop & Co. Messing- und Broncewarenfabrik" in Altena. The factory produced brassware for building materials. As a family operated company with tradition, the name Oventrop is at the heart of the brand and the company. The sixth-generation, tradition-rich company stands for competence and proximity to the customer.

Competent (leading in hydraulic systems and potable water hygiene), groundbreaking (we set standards with innovations), and especially personable (we are close to our customers like no one else). Oventrop sets standards through innovations and is a competence leader in hydraulic systems and potable water hygiene. For example, the groundbreaking dwelling station "Regudis W-HTE" has set the standard in terms of hydraulic key figures for an efficient and eco-friendly energy distribution throughout the house. In addition to highlights for hydronic balancing such as the AQ valve, Oventrop also holds a large number of active patent families.

The most important and well-known products are the Uni LH Thermostat, used in room climate, and the HydroControl double regulating and commissioning valve and Regudis dwelling station, both used in hydronic balancing. With these innovative and modular products and service, Oventrop pushes forward with energy transformation and is therefore actively contributing to climate targets. All products are of long-lasting quality, easy to install, save energy, and are able to be connected to flexible systems worldwide.

Visually, the company relies on uniform, distinctive, and therefore unmistakable brand characteristics. Through their logo, icon, the color cyan and an archetypal design, Oventrop products have qualities consistent with the brand. This strategy has paid off: no other company in the heating valve field has won more awards.

As with many medium-sized companies, Oventrop has also been presented with current global challenges such as digitalization and sustainability. The company began a large-scale brand relaunch project (Recreate) in 2018, in order to not only meet the changed conditions of the market, but to use them as an opportunity with a view to the future. The brand was comprehensively and holistically realigned (Transform) in their products and services, their design, and in terms of communication and brand behavior. The company is also driving digitalization, globalization, and sustainable action forward. In order to safeguard their German facilities and supply chains, as well as maintain the ability to compete on the market long-term, two additional international production locations have also been established.

The "human element" also plays an important role at Oventrop. More emphasis than ever is to be placed on corporate culture in order to increase competitiveness. A higher level of attractiveness as an employer will ensure employees and jobs in the Sauerland (be resilient).
Oventrop received two prestigious awards for its successful international brand relaunch in 2021: the German Brand Award in Gold and the German Brand Award in the category of "Brand Revival of the Year."

FACTS AND FIGURES

PRODUCTS
products for the areas of heating, cooling, and clean potable water, for example thermostats, hydraulic regulators and dwelling stations

LOCATIONS
numerous representatives worldwide and eight subsidiaries, among others in France, Great Britain, Poland, USA, and China

FOUNDER
Arnold Oventrop (1851, Altena)

OWNERS
families Rump and Fähnrich. Managing Directors are Jochen Fähnrich (since 2010) and Johannes Rump (since 2017).

EMPLOYEES
approx. 1,000 nationally, approx. 200 internationally (2022)

SALES
in Germany, sales are made in three stages via wholesalers (B2B); in other countries, such as China, there are direct sales (B2C)

WEBSITE
oventrop.com

Left: With their distinct and pure design, the ClimaCon F Room Thermostat blends in to any environment. Right: Regudis W-HTE Dwelling Stations can be expanded modularly and make the operation of heat pumps even more efficient.

WE REGULATE IT.
SINCE 1851.

Festo

AUTOMATION TECHNOLOGY
AND TECHNICAL TRAINING
AND EDUCATION

Originally founded in 1925 in Esslingen, Festo developed a complete product spectrum for mechanical engineering and equipment construction in the 1950s, with the help of pneumatics. That was the foundation for their new business division, Automation Technology, in which the independent, family-owned company, is now internationally successful in many sectors and industries.

Festo has a permanent offering of roughly 33,000 products and system solutions, as well as approximately 10,000 customer-specific solutions; and that's not counting the ready-to-install solutions and their related service offerings in factory and process automation.

Festo views itself as a teaching company, which doesn't only live continuing education and improvement itself, but also promotes a flexible and practical educational culture, so that customers and partners are future-oriented and current with the latest trends.

In 1965, the business division, Teaching Materials and Seminars, was established. Since then, Festo has developed didactic learning systems, training, and consulting for industrial companies and for vocational education and training in Germany. Currently, Festo Didactic offers the most modern qualification solutions for approximately 56,000 industrial companies and educational institutes all around the world.

In order to maximize productivity in factory and process automation for its customers, Festo creates new solutions day after day. Decisive for their success is not only the right technology, but also knowledge of the market, trends, and relevant industry issues. Festo offers up its expertise personally and close-by in the Festo Experience Centers (FECs), places for conversation, questions, the collaborative development of new approaches, and the testing of ideas.

The family-owned company places a high value on its independence and on long-term thinking and action, which gives its employees and its customers, partners, and suppliers security. Innovation is an important part of the company tradition, because requirements in their field change constantly. Seven percent of their annual turnover goes into research and development.

Their research approaches and projects are primarily related to the fields of biologization, artificial intelligence, and digital engineering. For example, research is being done to translate animal locomotion into machine locomotion. In robotics, Cobots (collaborative robots) are meant to relieve employees during strenuous or monotonous tasks, and make working easier and healthier. With the PhotoBionicCell, biomass can be cultivated in a closed cycle, an approach to climate-neutral production of starting materials for diverse industries.

The company is working on becoming climate neutral in the new few years, and wants to make a decisive contribution to improving the quality of life of current and future generations with its research and intelligent solutions for energy efficiency and CO_2 neutrality.

FACTS AND FIGURES

PRODUCTS
factory automation, process automation, LifeTech automation, digitalization, automation, training and consulting, technical education

LOCATIONS
more than 250 subsidiaries in 61 countries, authorized representatives in a further 40 countries, services in 176 countries

FOUNDER
Gottlieb Stoll (1925, Esslingen)

EMPLOYEES
20,700 worldwide (2021)

SALES
Australia, Africa, America, Asia, Europe; distribution follows via direct sales and Festo official partners (retailers)

WEBSITE
festo.com

FESTO

Fette Compacting

MECHANICAL ENGINEERING

The market for medicine and dietary supplements is booming
internationally. As a manufacturer of machines and tools for
the production of tablets, Fette Compacting contributes to
the success of their industry with innovative solutions.

The amount of prescription as well as non-prescription medicine has been increasing for years. In addition, there is an increasing number of dietary supplements. The classic tablet counts as one of the most popular forms of administration, since it is distinguished by its versatility, stability, and uncomplicated use: for the manufacturer, as well as the retailer and the user.

Since the development of the first tablet press in 1948, the brand Fette Compacting has evolved into one of the leading providers of tablet presses in the pharmaceutical industry worldwide, with more than 5,000 machines installed. From its factory in Schwarzenbek near Hamburg, Fette Compacting also supplies modern tableting tools and processing equipment all over the world and is available to it's customers for service, training, and consulting services.

With decades of experience, Fette Compacting has substantially influenced the industry. With the introduction of the high-speed tablet press P2000 in 1970 and the first computer-controlled tablet press internationally, the PT2080, as well as numerous technically revolutionary inventions and advancements, the company has made a decisive contribution to efficient and safe tablet production. In doing so, the subjects of containment and continuous manufacturing have been of particular interest during the development of new system solutions. Systems made by Fette Compacting make continuous manufacturing possible with compact, modular installation and easy to use systems. The results are an optimized production facility layout and simplification of the entire process chain: important prerequisites for a high production output with moderate investment and personnel costs as well as significantly lower space requirements.

As a family-owned company, Fette Compacting has been thinking and acting in a socially and ecologically responsible manner for generations, and relies on the synergy effects between economic goals and sustainability. As an example of this, the company was recognized in 2021 with an EcoVadis Label in Silver.

With their newest business unit, OSDi, the company is focusing on smart tools to further optimize production, ones that will focus on the most significant challenges of OSD producers: operate, maintain, train. With the help of digital solutions, knowledge and data can be used in a targeted way. Fette Compacting has developed solution-oriented applications for an efficient optimization of tablet production in close cooperation with its customers.

FACTS AND FIGURES

PRODUCTS
tablet presses, tableting tools, processing equipment as well as relevant service, training, and consulting services

LOCATIONS
Schwarzenbek near Hamburg (headquarters), Nanjing/China (technology and production location), centers of expertise and subsidiaries worldwide

FOUNDER
Wilhelm Fette
(1908, Hamburg-Altona)

MANAGING DIRECTORS
Joachim Dittrich (CEO)
and Anke Fischer (CFO)

EMPLOYEES
LMT Group approx. 1,800
(2021, among more than 20 locations of the LMT Group)

SALES
direct sales worldwide from Schwarzenbek and China

WEBSITE
fette-compacting.com

EFFICIENCY FOR PHARMA AND NUTRITION

Generic

ePAT

Fast Product Change Over

Modular

Compact

Tri-Easy

Operator Safety

The FE CPS is the most advanced solution on the market for continuous dosing and mixing of raw materials, including conveying and feeding the high-quality mixture into all subsequent powder processing equipment.

mawa

DESIGNER LIGHTS AND LIGHTING
SYSTEMS, CUSTOMIZED LIGHTS,
AND LIGHT PLANNING

With their visionary lighting system, mawa has set the standard in the field of lighting for decades. The company is exemplary in terms of design quality and sustainable production.

Credit: Martin Tervoort

For more than 40 years, mawa has created highly sophisticated lights and lighting solutions for historical monuments, art shows, and significant architectural projects. The lights created by the manufacturer from the Brandenburg municipality of Seddiner See are also represented in renowned collections such as that of the Museum of Modern Art in New York. The solid understanding of design that the company possesses is exemplified in the excellent workmanship of their products, their technical finesse, and their own 27 design protection registrations. All mawa luminaires are originals that were developed and produced at the Seddiner location, from the first sketches to the production-ready product. The international team works with a state-of-the-art tool and machine plant. In order to implement the company's own lighting design as precisely as possible, employees install the luminaire systems directly in the building.

The brand name mawa consists of the first two letters of the name Martin Wallroth, who founded the company in 1977 in Berlin-Kreuzberg. As a visionary in light design and the application of technically demanding system lighting, he was formative in his company for decades, which won numerous international design awards. In the early days, the mawa designs often took on a pioneering role. Starting in the 1980s, the manufacturer began to collaborate with well-known designers. He started to create custom designed lights early on, going above and beyond his standard product portfolio; for example, for the Federal Chancellor's office, the Ministry of Economics, the Corbusierhaus, as well at the Maxim-Gorki-Theater in Berlin and the Lutherhaus in Wittenberg. A strategic re-orientation followed in 2002, and since then the focus has been on designer lights and lighting systems. In 2021, Martin Wallroth handed mawa over to the PROLED GROUP. Today, Peter Gawlik and Christian von Sassen are responsible for the management and focus of the company.

mawa considers its most important product to be the "wittenberg 4.0;" no other lighting series is easier to customize or has as many variations. The multifunctional light head has been technologically advanced and formally redesigned over the course of its fourth-generation design. The result is a reduced luminaire volume with a slim and delicate design that offers better light. That is how the compact measurements of the wittenberg 4.0 are able to save valuable centimeters, which make a subtle difference in the quality of the architectural design and optimal lighting planning. The light is compelling everywhere where spotlights are used as a design medium due to its simple, aesthetic housing, which is used without visible cables or screws.

mawa would like to continue to establish itself as the partner for anyone who loves and wants to understand good light. For this reason, the company has evolved into a high-quality producer of technically functional as well as decoratively sophisticated light. Innovation and professional manufacturing are of primary importance. mawa has successfully held their ground on the market by modernizing their systems for production, logistics, and installation, as well as focusing on a European network of delivery companies. Short delivery routes as well as the knowledge of where parts and components have come from are important to the lighting specialist. Upcycling and repairs are taken into account during the development of new products. All of these factors combined should make the company even more sustainable.

It's not only about rethinking, changing, and making their own production and actions fit for the future; mawa is also constantly reflecting on itself in order to move, "one step smarter" into the future.

FACTS AND FIGURES

PRODUCTS
designer lights and lighting systems, customized lights, and light planning

LOCATIONS
Seddiner See (production) and Michendorf (administration), Brandenburg

FOUNDER
Martin Wallroth (1977, Berlin-Kreuzberg)

OWNER
PROLED GROUP

EMPLOYEES
67 (2022)

SALES
worldwide; particularly in Germany, Austria, Switzerland, Italy, and Greece through specialty stores and project leaders from the fields of architecture, light planning and interior design

WEBSITE
mawa-design.de

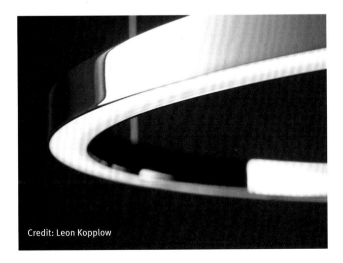

Credit: Leon Kopplow

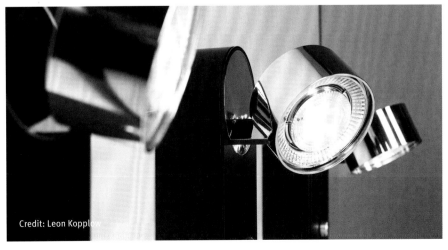

Credit: Leon Kopplow

SLOWLI Concept

INTERIOR / FURNITURE AND ACCESSORIES

The most important place of refuge for most people is their own home. With sustainably produced furniture and living accessories made from natural materials, SLOWLI Concept is designed to create a true haven within your own four walls.

CONSCIOUS LIVING
AND SUSTAINABLE
LIVING

Unsurprisingly, according to statistics, people spend the largest portion of their time at home. In fact, current studies show that the time spent inside one's own four walls has markedly increased over recent years. The significance of the home environment for well-being is correspondingly high. At the same time, sustainability and environmental protection don't only begin at your front door, but behind it. SLOWLI Concept from South Tyrol combines these two aspects of living — the need to have a soothing retreat and the interest in a responsible approach to the environment — by producing natural and sustainable furniture and living accessories.

The longing for more sustainable living, the interest in Slow Living and a love for details and her home in South Tyrol motivated interior designer Angelika Frenademetz to found SLOWLI Concept in 2020. Since then, the young start-up company has created furniture and accessories with the clear goal of bringing a country idyll to the city.

Solid wood furniture, wool blankets and pillows, as well as ceramic plates from the SLOWLI Concept Interior Design Studio are produced according to traditional craftsmanship. This generates long-lasting, customizable products, such as bedroom furniture — wooden beds and beds made of Swiss stone pine wood for a sense of well-being in the bedroom — from natural, regional raw materials: textiles, ceramics, wood, wool from South Tyrol sheep, as well as recycled materials.

The acronym SLOW was composed by SLOWLI Concept from the main aspects of its own understanding of sustainability: "Sustainable, Local, Organic, Whole," describes how the founder has implemented her own sustainable Slow Living philosophy.

SLOWLI Concept produces furniture pieces and accessories that are truly handmade in collaboration with local manufacturers, social workshops and freelance artists and designers — sustainable, minimalistic, attentive. Nature and design are always in harmony, for conscious living and a home to arrive at.

Products from SLOWLI Concept are sustainable particularly through their durability and longevity. These quality aspects turn furniture pieces and accessories into long-standing companions that are able to look back on an even longer life thanks to the use of recycled raw materials. SLOWLI Concept aims to impress not only through its quality, but also by offering showpieces with which customers consciously decide against fast-moving consumer behavior.

With this philosophy, SLOWLI Concept has presented itself as a young company with growth potential. The fact that the South Tyroleans are on the right track has also been confirmed by awards such as the German Design Award 2022 in the category of ECO-Design and being chosen as a Green Product Award Winner 2022.

FACTS AND FIGURES

PRODUCTS
sustainable furniture and accessories

LOCATION
Bozen, South Tyrol

FOUNDER/OWNER
Angelika Frenademetz (2020)

EMPLOYEES
less than 5 (2022)

SALES
direct sales via an online shop and retailers

WEBSITE
slowliconcept.com

Credit: Alex Moling

153

bullmer

CUTTING SOLUTIONS FOR
THE TEXTILE PROCESSING
INDUSTRY

For more than 60 years, bullmer has
produced specialized machines for cutting
textiles. The company has a decisive
advantage in their industry as a
full-service provider.

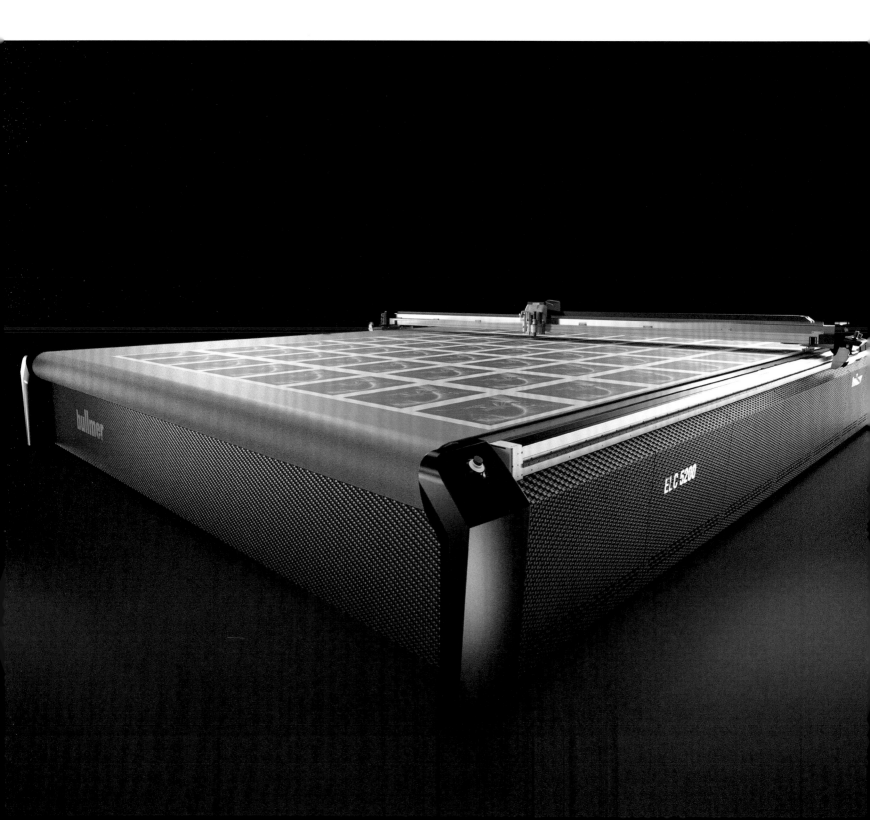

From fashion textiles and upholstery fabric, to rugs, to foam and composite materials: bullmer is an innovative mechanical engineering company that develops and produces all necessary machines for cutting and layering technology. One of the most significant strengths of the company lies in the construction of special purpose machines as well as the production and manufacture of complete system lines for the processing of textile and flexible materials. Internationally, there is no competitor that can claim a similar product depth. The portfolio of the mechanical engineering company from Mehrstetten, in Baden-Württemberg, encompasses single and high layer cutters, spreading machines, material handling, CAD, in-house production as well as consulting for the textile processing industry. The most important product currently is the single layer cutter, "Premiumcut ELC."

Karl Bullmer founded his company in 1933 as a metal factory producing in Mehrstetten, in the Swabian Jura. The serial production of cutting and spreading devices began toward the end of the 1950s. Over the following years, the production range was expanded more and more and by 1975 it was already being successfully sold in more than 60 countries. Today, bullmer holds the rights to more than 100 patents and employs experienced staff who have been with the company for a long time. In addition, the company provides training for its own qualified future employees in order to be able to continue producing successfully in the future.

bullmer continues to offer the entire product range for the process chain, "textile cutting for flexible parts," in many industrial sectors. In addition, bullmer creates supply systems with various loading and laying devices, transport systems, and cutting systems with the appropriate software for the handling and processing of textile materials. Due to its advanced existing sales and development department, bullmer is in the position to respond dynamically to new market requirements and specific customer requests. This is how customized cutting systems are created for an optimal production process at the customer's location. This also allows specific requirements for new markets to be met and fulfilled quickly.

The trend of moving the textile processing industry back to European manufacturing locations has benefited the tradition-rich company bullmer. This is because the highly successful, sustainable, and efficient production of special purpose machines still takes place exclusively in the Swabian Jura. It is no wonder that the manufacturer is optimistic about the future.

FACTS AND FIGURES

PRODUCTS
cutting solutions for the textile processing industry

LOCATION
Mehrstetten, in the Swabian Jura

FOUNDER
Karl Bullmer (1933, Mehrstetten)

OWNER
New Jack Sewing Machine, China

EMPLOYEES
150 (2022, in Germany)

SALES
worldwide

WEBSITE
bullmer.de

emens

TECHNOLOGY FOR INDUSTRY, INFRASTRUC-
TURE, MOBILITY, AND HEALTH

As a company focused on technology, Siemens unites real and
digital worlds — and in doing so, helps their customers to
transform their industries and markets and therefore improve
daily life for billions of people.

SIEMENS XCELERATOR

Accelerate
your digital
transformation

A Berlin rear courtyard, 175 years ago: that is where the history of a company began, on October 12, 1847, that would not only create technical history, but would also revolutionize daily life for billions of people all over the world. Siemens AG: a technology company with a focus on the fields of industry, infrastructure, mobility, and health — from resource-efficient factories, intelligent buildings and power grids to low-emission trains and advanced healthcare. Everything began on the small side, as a start-up. Up until the mid-19th century, messages could only be sent via the traditional routes, for example with the help of an optical telegraph, a courier, or a stagecoach. Everything changed fundamentally with the electric telegraph. Werner von Siemens made a significant contribution to the development of new technology by recognizing technical deficiencies in the construction of existing electric telegraph apparatuses- and developing his own pointer telegraph. Electrical telegraphy stands for the beginning of the compression of space and time. It brought people together and heralded the arrival of information exchanges across countries and continents. 175 years later, the ten-man operation has become a global player that continues to play a decisive role in shaping the history of innovation and technology over time. Today, the Siemens concern is one of the largest companies in Germany, with an annual turnover of 62.3 billion euros in fiscal year 2021, and a leading technology company worldwide. Siemens has revolutionized various branches with technological developments, and has set the course for the future. In June 2022, the open digital business platform Siemens Xcelerator was presented to the public. With that, the digital transformation will be accelerated and innovations expedited more quickly. In order to overcome the challenges of our time, such as increasing geopolitical tensions, the climate crisis, and the pandemic, we need a common goal, teamwork, and the latest technologies. That is why the Siemens modular portfolio encompasses Xcelerator Services, software, and IoT-compatible hardware from Siemens and certified partners. This ecosystem continuously grows and includes partners of every size: from independent solution providers up to hyperscalers. At the same time, the technical principles are groundbreaking: all products are or will be designed to be interoperable, flexible, open, cyber-secure and available as a service. That means that the hardware and software portfolio will be modular, connected to the Cloud, and provided with standard programming interfaces to enable customers, partners, and developers to create their own personalized solutions. Hardware can be continually improved and upgraded with new software. Customers will be able to more easily combine, integrate, and adapt technologies. And on the constantly evolving marketplace, customers, partners, and developers can search for solutions together, exchange ideas, develop them, and ultimately attain them. In this way digital transformations can be made simpler, faster, and more scalable. Digitalization, transformation, and the Siemens guiding principle, "Transforming the everyday to create a better tomorrow," is also reflected in their communication and positions Siemens as a brand that has innovation embedded in its essence and spearheads change. Simple, flexible graphics, customer-centric imagery, as well as an emotional and engaging language are present throughout their website. The communication is simple, optimistic, and personable and built on three main principles: clarity, purpose, and effect.

The new appearance of the digital business platform Siemens Xcelerator was first displayed during its launch in June.Standard in its appearance is the new X form, based on the fundamental Siemens Xcelerator idea: IT meets OT. It also stands for the moment of acceleration when both elements come together, creating a striking, simple graphic in different combinations, a consistent look across all touchpoints.

FACTS AND FIGURES

PRODUCTS
technology solutions with a focus on industry, infrastructure, mobility and health

LOCATIONS
Berlin, Munich, 125 further locations in Germany, 190 subsidiaries worldwide

FOUNDER
Werner von Siemens (1847, Berlin)

OWNER
Stock Company

EMPLOYEES
305,000 (2021)

SALES
worldwide

WEBSITE
siemens.com

Let's accelerate digital transformation; easier and faster.

ZWIESEL

GLASS INDUSTRY

Sounds like Zwiesel: for 150 years, Zwiesel glasses have embellished celebrations and pleasurable moments with elegant shapes and extraordinary sound. "I recognize our glasses by their sound," the statement made by a Zwiesel glassmaker didn't become the slogan of the tradition-rich company, which celebrated its anniversary in 2022, for no reason.

Credit: Ingo Peters

Zwiesel Glass has mastered several crises and challenges since 1872, when it was founded as a glasswork called, "Annathal," by Anton Müller. Ownership structure, production facilities, and employees were the basis of a sometimes-turbulent evolution. Up until it was taken over in 2001 by Dr. Robert Hartel and Prof. Dr. Andreas Buske, the company had been part of the Schott Concern for decades. Finally, Zwiesel Glass was again a family-owned company, and the brand was reorganized during its new beginning. Shortly thereafter, a quantum leap in crystal glass manufacturing was performed with the introduction of Tritan® crystal glass. "We can do brilliance, we can do transparency, dishwasher-safe, scratch resistant, and design: we live glass. We were proud to show this off and it was well-received on the market," summarized Andreas Buske, today the sole managing director and proprietor. The conviction that they could become the world market leader in glassware with the best manufacturing and craftsmanship was rewarded. Today, Zwiesel Glass is a leader in the luxury hotels and gastronomy segment.

Zwiesel Glass set standards in design as well. The drinking glass Pure was groundbreaking when it was brought out in 2005, with its striking contour at the base of the glass, and is still a bestseller today. On the occasion of the anniversary, two exclusive series were created with the multi-award-winning designer Sebastian Herkner — one of which was the five-piece series Journey, where the unique stems visualize the milestones of 150 years of history.

Success and quality standards are binding. The company has always been responsible with resources and the environment. Sustainability is a major subject, which is reflected in every glass as roughly 50 % of every individual glass is made from recycled Tritan® crystal glass. In 2021, the production was converted to oxy-fuel combustion technology, which significantly reduces carbon dioxide and nitrogen oxide emissions and decreases energy use by 30 percent.

With the new renaming and brand relaunch in 2020, tradition and modernity were united and a solid basis for the future was created. The reference to Zwiesel, its place of origin, represents pride in the company's heritage, in its long experience as a foundation for excellence in material technology and craftsmanship, and for the ability — as proven more than once — to keep breaking new ground and adapt to the spirt of the times, despite tradition.

This has been shown by the recognition of the German Brand Award for outstanding branding work. Numerous series from Zwiesel Glass, whether handmade or machine produced, have been awarded prestigious design prizes such as the German Brand Award and the Red Dot Award, and many more distinctions.

FACTS AND FIGURES

PRODUCTS
glasses, glassware and accessories

LOCATIONS
Zwiesel (Germany), Halimba (Hungary), Barcelona (Spain), Shanghai (China), Tokyo (Japan), USA, Mumbai (India)

FOUNDER
Anton Müller (1872, Zwiesel)

OWNER AND CHAIRMAN OF THE BOARD
Prof. Dr. Andreas Buske

EMPLOYEES
500 worldwide (2022)

SALES
in more than 130 countries in Europe, USA, South America, Asia-Pacific as well as the Near and Middle East and Africa. Direct sales also via wholesalers and retailers

WEBSITE
zwiesel.de

ZWIESEL GLAS

Grohe AG

PLUMBING INDUSTRY

Over more than seven decades, the brand GROHE has been successful in becoming a synonym for high quality bathroom fittings. With a unique design language, the so-called GROHE DNA, they have been successful in connecting recognizability and innovation.

Credit: Grohe AG

With innovative fittings, Grohe provides an important service in designing a custom bathroom. GROHE views their portfolio as one element in a distinctive water experience and as a contribution to the perfect "me-moment" for health and personal wellness.

Three key elements give GROHE products a consistent design and therefore an ideal recognition value. GROHE views the stringent combination of the characteristic GROHE ring, the adherence to the seven-degree rule as well as the lozenge (an oval design form) as part of its DNA. The ring indicates the intended use of the product, is related to the function and should serve as an orientation point for the user. The angle of the handles and the spout are set at a precise seven degrees. Based on research findings, this slight bend is meant to additionally improve the user experience. As an inviting element, the shape of the lozenge underlines the "sensual minimalism" of GROHE's design philosophy.

Although high demand and numerous awards might suggest it, GROHE is not resting on the success of its products, some of which are already iconic. With a view to the individual needs of its customers and with strict use of their unique design language, GROHE dares to reinterpret already established product lines. The reinvention of GROHE Allure from their premium portfolio is a prominent example. With the new Allure line of fittings, GROHE holds onto the idea of the timeless aesthetic on one side, while also offering a contemporary option to turn a bathroom into a personal home spa.

As a result of this demanding task, the new fitting series Allure offers the perfect balance between precise proportions and refined surface finishes. The connection between the most modern water technology and German craftsmanship in the three-hole version from Allure offers a unique highlight with its haptic feedback. As part of the GROHE Spa Collection, the Allure fittings offer a harmonious bathroom design according to the individual's style thanks to their different colors and finishes, perfectly matched to the GROHE Allure accessories.

"Our strength is that we delve deep into the hearts of our customers, observe people and their behaviors, and understand human needs and different cultures. Our in-house design team is able to apply our unique GROHE design language and transform this knowledge into useful products that reflect our brand values." (Patrick Speck, Leader LIXIL Global Design, EMENA)

FACTS AND FIGURES

PRODUCTS
plumbing and kitchen solutions

LOCATION
Hemer (Nordrhein-Westfalen)

FOUNDER
Friedrich Grohe (1936, Hemer)

OWNER
the company GROHE has belonged to the Japanese LIXIL Group since 2014

EMPLOYEES
approx. 7,000 in 150 countries, 2,600 in Germany (2022)

SALES
plumbing wholesalers and retail stores, online stores, showrooms for installers, architects, designers, and end consumers

WEBSITE
grohe.de

GROHE SPA

LEONHARD KURZ Stiftung & Co. KG

CHEMICAL INDUSTRY

The fifth-generation owner-operated business develops and manufactures decorative and functional coatings that are applied to carrier foils and employed for a wide-variety of products. Almost everyone could have had a product with a KURZ coating in their hand at one time, as the spectrum of the worldwide leading company for thin film technology is wide and can be used with automotive components, cell phones, TVs, washing machines, furniture, packaging, books, textiles, bottle labels, bank cards, and much more.

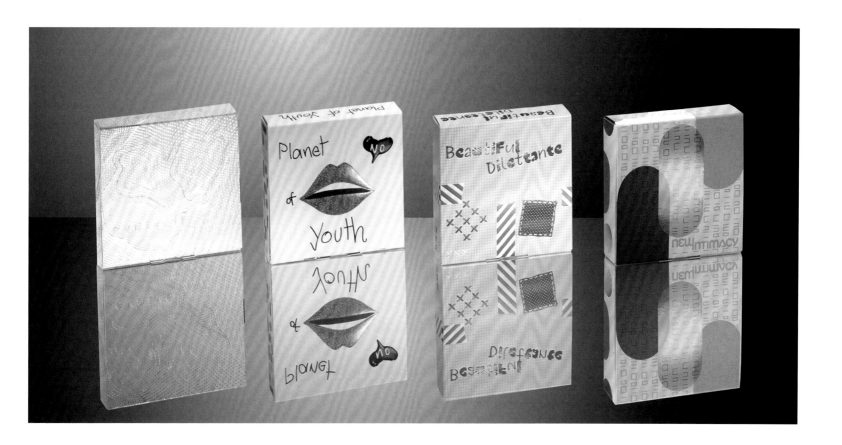

The customers are just as varied as the products and solutions. Processors, printers, brand manufacturers, designers, original equipment manufacturers, and even entire governments allow KURZ to decorate products, enhance brands, label goods, protect surfaces or prevent counterfeiting. In addition, KURZ links the visual world with the virtual world by adding digital functions to visual elements.

KURZ offers complete solutions including project consulting, machine technology, and tool technology. The KURZ Group is present in more than 30 locations worldwide and manufactures in Europe, Asia and the USA according to uniform quality and environmental standards. A global network of subsidiaries, representatives and sales offices provides for short routes, reliable deliveries and individual support on location.

The company has four divisions: packaging and print (graphic industry), plastic decoration (automotive, home appliances, sensor technology, etc.), security (trademark protection, decoration, bank notes, ID-documents, etc.) and applications (machine technology, stamp technology, in-house engineering, etc.).

All KURZ products specialize in surfaces. Every design possesses and requires a surface where the design and material used are as versatile as the product itself: smooth, raw, soft touch, with or without texture, backlit or with a function. The most important thing is that the surface tells a story and makes every product unique and able to be experienced.

Even digital solutions are related to surfaces. For example, programs calculate the optimal use of a print sheet or the perfect layout of a stamp. Holograms with interactive elements, application programs, product coding; all of these require a surface. In 2016, the KURZ business group founded KURZ DIGITAL SOLUTIONS, in order to advise companies in all digital stages and to support technological changes. Those products include the Visible Digital Seal, for example, which protects physical and digital documents from misuse, or Easy Service, which bundles all services related to a product in one code.

One of the secret's to KURZ's success is certainly that the company continues to reinvent itself, and does so out of its own convictions and not necessity. Since its founding, they have focused on innovation and the ambition to keep pace

with the times, in order to give their clients a competitive advantage in their own markets. Existing solutions are continuously improved in order to optimize their workmanship, achieve process stability and security for their production, and to guarantee their economic stability and future. In addition to that, KURZ produces worldwide according to the same standards and with the same raw materials in order to be able to guarantee consistent color, quality, and reliability everywhere.

The family-owned business also cares strongly about the topic of sustainability. They have been manufacturing according to the highest standards for decades and work as sustainably as possible.

New solutions continue to improve the sustainability of the products. The option to recycle products decorated by KURZ remains unchanged, and the way they are sorted is not impacted by their coating. This has been checked through multiple tests and has been confirmed by the INGEDE Certificate, for example. Some finishes are even compostable.

Large investments have been made, especially over the past five years, in new processes for recycling, waste air disposal, energy saving, and regeneration, as well as in the alignment of KURZ products with environmental sustainability.

A large part of the high amount of energy required to run the plastic processing company comes from its own photovoltaic plant. Today, the amount of CO_2 emissions has been reduced 50 percent. Since 2021 LEONHARD KURZ has also been part of the initiative for corporate sustainability from the UN Global Compact for an inclusive, sustainable global economy. The market leader in thin foil technology is aware of its global responsibility and wants to preserve the natural balance for future generations and protect the environment as it is the basis of all our lives.

FACTS AND FIGURES

PRODUCTS
decorative and functional coatings applied to carrier foils for a variety of products (thin film technology)

LOCATIONS
domestic: Fürth, Döbeln, Sulzbach-Rosenberg
international (subsidiaries and representatives): Argentina, Australia, Austria, Benelux, Brazil, Canada, Chile, Columbia, Croatia, Cyprus, Czech Republic / Slovak Republic, Denmark, Great Britain, Hong Kong, Hungary, India, Indonesia, Ireland, Iceland, Israel, Italy, Japan, Lebanon, Malaysia, Mexico, North Africa, Norway, Peru, Poland, Portugal, Sweden, Switzerland, Singapore, Slovenia, Spain, South Africa, South Korea, Taiwan, Thailand, Turkey, United Arab Emirates, Ukraine, USA, Venezuela, Vietnam

FOUNDER
Leonhard Kurz (1899)

OWNERS
Walter and Peter Kurz

EMPLOYEES
approx. 5,500 (2022)

SALES
worldwide via subsidiaries and representatives abroad

WEBSITE
kurz.de

MAKING
EVERY PRODUCT
UNIQUE

Design changes our behavior and our actions.

PROF. MIKE RICHTER

WAGNER

CONSUMER GOODS MANUFACTURER

Unexpected events lead to being unexpectedly creative. The Black Forest think tank has reconsidered — and rebuilt.

WIR SCHAFFEN GROSSES.

Under the motto: "We're growing. We need more space. We create big things.," Wagner invested approximately six million euros in an ambitious building project. The new Wagner-Werk 3 factory is climate friendly and resource-saving. Its energy comes from a photovoltaic system on top of the entire roof. It is heated with a heat pump and concrete core activation as well as a ventilation system with heat recovery. In short, the building is practically self-sufficient; the use of fossil fuels can be almost completely avoided. "If energy costs hit the roof, it'll be better for us to make our energy ourselves," summarized Ellen Wagner, who leads the company together with her brother Ulrich Wagner. But it wasn't only rising energy costs that contributed to the decision to put on a 2,150 square meter building addition. Wagner has continually grown over the past years; a successful "global player" has grown out of the founders' small start-up.

Under the umbrella brand, "WAGNER design yourself," Wagner develops and produces elegant and functional products for the home, garden, workshop, and office. Furniture glides, for example. But not just any furniture glides: the founder Roland Wagner redesigned these small but indispensable components for modern furniture design more than twenty years ago- and made them internationally successful under the brand QuickClick®. More than 2,000 variations of the gliding innovation have been created out of the original two models, repeatedly rewarded for design, innovation, and sustainability, and true problem solvers for furniture manufacturers and users. This is because QuickClick® is the first furniture glider system with changeable glide and stop inserts for every kind of furniture and every kind of floor covering.

The concept is as simple as it is ingenious: for every QuickClick® variation, a base element is permanently fixed to the furniture and a compatible insert or attachment is clicked in or out of it. In the event of wear or a change in flooring, the elements can be changed out or turned over in seconds. This intelligent idea makes the QuickClick® system extremely easy to maintain, an important aspect for objects especially. Simplicity is king in terms of customer service as well. "If there's wear and tear or the flooring has been changed, the furniture manufacturers don't need to find the correct QuickClick® replacement inserts for the user as they are available to purchase directly from us in the Wagner online shop. Very simple," Ulrich Wagner explained the clever concept.

FACTS AND FIGURES

PRODUCTS
furniture components, living accessories, transport helpers, plant trolleys

LOCATION
Lahr (Black Forest)

FOUNDER
Roland Wagner (1977)

OWNERS
Ellen Wagner and Ulrich Wagner

EMPLOYEES
200

SALES
worldwide via furniture manufacturers, large and small retail stores, e-commerce

WEBSITE
wagner-systeme.de

design yourself
WAGNER®

Two of the many QuickClick® variations: this is the ultra-flat "Silencer Slim." Due to its minimal height, it is practically invisible in the context of the furniture design. An integrated sound absorber muffles disruptive noises and vibrations.

The "PIEDI Equalizer 2.0," developed especially for ergonomic sitting, contains a specialized spring. Seating furniture that has been equipped with the novel comfort component actively follows the movements of the seated person.

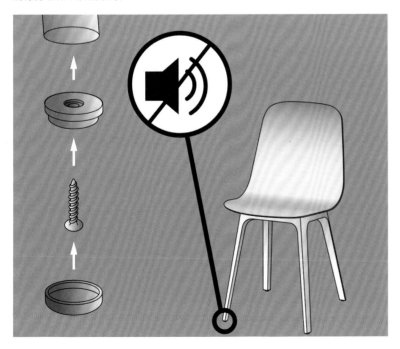

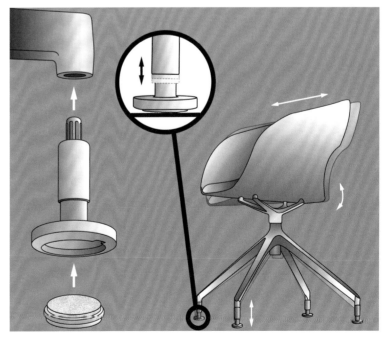

Poggenpohl

Inventor oft he modern kitchen for 130 years

INTERIORS, KITCHEN MANUFACTURER

Poggenpohl has a long tradition of innovation. When Friedemir Poggenpohl founded the family business in 1892, his aim was "to improve the kitchen". Over the past 130 years, the small cabinetmaker's shop has evolved into the leading brand for German-made luxury kitchen architecture. As the inventor of the modern kitchen, Poggenpohl today sustainably combines architectural concepts and applications with trendsetting design, superb craftmanship and technical precision.

For Poggenpohl, kitchens symbolise a life of enjoyment that is rich in character and full of energy. Kitchens are where people cook, celebrate, work and live – with fullness and enthusiasm. Thus, people are at the centre of the planning when Poggenpohl's architects develop custom solutions for their customers' individual ideas and living spaces. Each kitchen is a contemporary original, distinctively playing upon the surrounding architecture. Fascinating proportions, carefully selected quality materials and inspiring colours are combined in refreshing and consistently elegant interpretations.

The production in Germany ensures the quality and distinctiveness of the kitchens. The kitchens are manufactured at the company's headquarters in Herford, Germany, with the highest level of craftmanship and precision. The kitchens are sold in more than 70 countries worldwide via an international network of the company's own studios and authorised business partners.

KITCHEN ARCHITECTURE
SINCE 1892

FACTS AND FIGURES

PRODUCTS
customized kitchen architecture

LOCATION
Herford (headquarters)

FOUNDER
Friedemir Poggenpohl
(1892, Bielefeld)

OWNER
CEO Dirk Lange
Jomoo Group

EMPLOYEES
475 (2019)

WEBSITE
poggenpohl.com

Ronnefeldt

FOOD PRODUCTS / LUXURY FOOD

Excellent tea quality from the best tea gardens in the world has led Ronnefeldt through two eventful centuries. The name Ronnefeldt still stands for excellent tea quality, the finest enjoyment, and passion for the natural product tea today.

Tea made its way to Europe roughly 400 years ago. Almost another two centuries had passed before it came to Germany. At that point, it didn't take long before the hot drink had found its fans in every level of society.

Opening a teahouse in Frankfurt am Main, far away from the large German harbors, was a bold step in 1823. Today, in the 200th year of their success story, that decision was just the first of many countless challenges that made the family-owned company Ronnefeldt into what it is today: one of the leading tea brands worldwide in the sector of luxury hotels and food service. With the success of the tea, the young company was able to build Ronnefeldt into a brand whose popularity was reflected in its global market presence in little more than two decades.

The key to the success of the company, and the Ronnefeldt brand, was and is their focus on customers from the luxury hotel and food service sectors. Green and black tea from the best tea production regions in the world, herbal and fruit teas, and personal consulting and customer education for a holistic tea concept: Ronnefeldt helps its partners in the fields of food service and hospitality to be successful and viewed as the perfect hosts. The company has distinguished itself by stringently following the same strategy for two centuries, which is based on orientation of values, long-term planning, and sustainable work practices.

The subject of sustainability in particular has increased in meaning for Ronnefeldt over the past few years. For more than ten years, the tea experts have followed a tea-specific and regional approach which is focused on the working and living conditions of the people who live in the tea countries of origin. To do that, the company works with the organizations Childaid Network and Ethical Tea Partnership, which are committed to socially and ecologically sustainable business practices on location. Part of Ronnefeldt's ecologically sustainable strategy is also the step-by-step switch over to sustainable packing materials. To produce the best quality tea, teas are processed exclusively according to the Ronnefeldt quality philosophy which follows traditional, orthodox methods: hand-picked by following the principle, "two leaves and one bud," and processed carefully, not industrially. To do this, the five characteristic steps are performed during a time-consuming process: withering, rolling, fermenting, drying, and sorting.

They remain equally focused on a sophisticated look as well as a functional and practical approach for the packaging design. Ronnefeldt is continuously working on solutions for customers in the food service and hospitality industries in particular that simplify the work processes in tea preparation and service.

The tea competence gained over decades is passed on through seminars from the Ronnefeldt TeaAcademy®. Here, tea stockists and the people responsible for the tea service in food service and hospitality can be qualified as tea experts.

FACTS AND FIGURES

PRODUCTS
tea, tea concepts for luxury hotels and food service, services, tea seminars

LOCATIONS
Frankfurt am Main, Worpswede (near Bremen)

FOUNDER
Johann Tobias Ronnefeldt (1823, Frankfurt am Main)

OWNER
Jan-Berend Holzapfel

EMPLOYEES
130–140 (2022)

SALES
direct sales (DACH region), sales partner in more than 80 countries worldwide

WEBSITE
ronnefeldt.com

Ronnefeldt
TEA EXCELLENCE SINCE 1823

TEA EXCELLENCE SINCE 1823

Sustainably packaged organic product line 100 percent.

Hand-picked tea from the best tea gardens in the world.

Nurus

DESIGNER OFFICE FURNITURE

DESIGNING FOR
TOMORROW, IMPLE-
MENTING TODAY.

Founded in 1927, Nurus serves customers in more than 50 global locations by linking technology to its innovative design and giving priority to people's well-being. Nurus' advanced technologies and award-winning products that compound aesthetics and functionality emerge by considering the balance of technology, nature, and design.

The working environment has changed rapidly and fundamentally by comparison of the past decades. We do not use offices for one or two persons or closed doors anymore. The greatest need for today's working culture is a functional and private space for private calls, videoconferences, touchdown teamwork, spontaneous meetings, concentrated working or just resting. Nurus designed and developed Calma acoustic pods that set an international standard with their physical data.

Calma offers a location of quietness in crowded and noisy spaces such as open-plan offices and common areas, creates a zone of concentration and relaxation and relieves undisturbed cooperation and communication.

With Nurus Links® connection Calma also supports the use of mobile devices and laptops. The Calma Application that works integrated with Nurus Links®, helps you to find available Calmas, reserve it and send notifications to the attendees. Also with its smart software, you can control the sit-stand desk by your setting, the illumination level, and ventilation.

FACTS AND FIGURES

LOCATION
Munich

FOUNDER
founding year 1927

WEBSITE
nurus.de

nurus

P+L Innovations – trivida

DETACHABLE WHEELCHAIR WHEEL FOR MORE ACCESSIBILITY

The revolutionary trivida wheel makes it possible
for people in wheelchairs to have a life with more
independence and dignity. The innovative brand
stands for inclusion and the removal of barriers.

P ionieering solutions related to accessibility in a wheelchair: the brand trivida, from the development company, P+L Innovations, took on the task of removing barriers in some way, in order to make a more independent life possible for people in wheelchairs. With the innovative trivida wheelchair wheel, the company from Bad Krozingen, in Baden-Württemberg, was successful in creating a groundbreaking example of German engineering, which improves the quality of life for wheelchair users, family members, and professional caregivers.

Countless situations in daily life demand a change in position from wheelchair users. The detachable wheel allows those affected to transfer to and from their wheelchairs in an energy-saving, barrier-free way. To do so, the wheelchair is parked parallel to the desired location and is locked in place. Next, the upper segment of the wheel is unlocked and removed with the help of an ergonomic quick-release lever. That way, the person can slide onto the sofa or a bed securely and barrier-free. People that have movement limitations in their upper bodies may still require support, but no longer need to be lifted up.

The story of the brand, trivida, began a few decades ago. Even as a student, Christian Czapek was in pursuit of his vision to significantly optimize the construction of a wheelchair. The subject hit home again for the university-educated (diplom) designer many years later, when Czapek's brother became reliant on a wheelchair. He was unable to shake his idea until he reinvented the wheel, in the literal sense. He was successful in constructing a stable wheelchair wheel that could be detached into three large segments and therefore easily dismantled.

In 2019, the owners of the family-owned company P+L Innovations recognized the unique potential of the invention. Over the course of their collaboration, a specialist team contributed their particular expertise, innovative ideas, and technological improvements to its further development. From the first prototype to the series production of the revolutionary wheelchair wheel, every detail was minutely considered and tailor-made to the needs of the wheelchair-user.

The robust trivida wheel with intelligent triatec®-Technology is manufactured in Germany from high-quality, long-lasting materials and is compelling with its modern, functional design. In order to maintain the highest quality standards, the trivida-team works precisely and conscientiously according to medical guidelines such as the European Medical Device Regulations. Due to the Corona pandemic, the introduction of the wheel onto the market could not take place as planned; instead, the team had to be reduced and initial sales delayed until the end of 2021. The difficult time that was experienced together led to a strong cohesion among the team.

Viewing things from a different perspective, in order to develop new solutions, is trivida's method. Further innovative product solutions for wheelchair users are already in development, so that people who use wheelchairs are able to get more out of life.

FACTS AND FIGURES

PRODUCTS
detachable wheelchair wheel for more accessibility

LOCATION
Bad Krozingen

FOUNDERS
the Pflaumbaum family
(2019, Bad Krozingen)

OWNERS
the Pflaumbaum family

EMPLOYEES
8 (2022)

SALES
Europe and Australia

WEBSITE
trivida-info.com

Talkwalker

Talkwalker is an industry leader in the field of consumer intelligence and makes it possible for brands to build a close relationship with their users. The platform combines market leading social analytics and AI technology with expertise related to unstructured data as well as a global team of insight analysts and data storytellers. Top brands and agencies worldwide use Talkwalker, thanks to its data coverage in 187 languages.

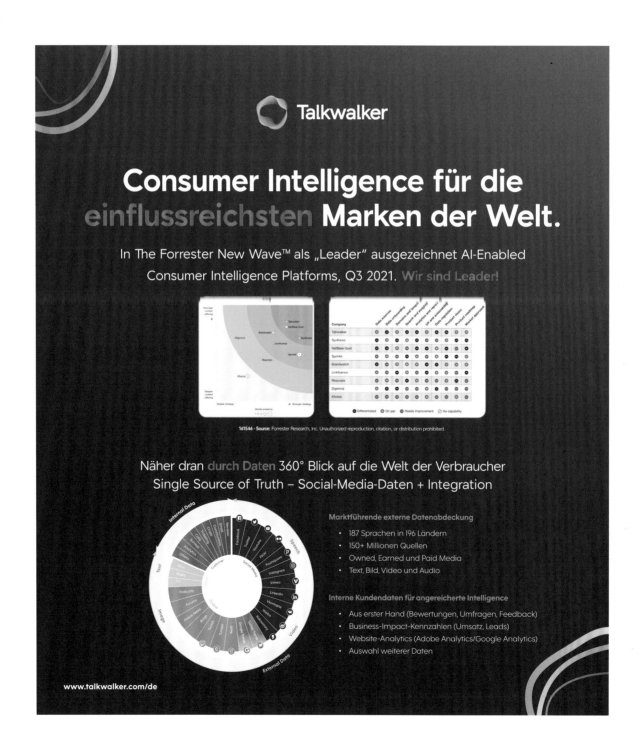

The goal of the company founded in Luxembourg in 2019 by Christophe Folschette and Thibaut Britz was, "To walk through the talk;" to understand the meaning behind all words and symbols and to help people to make sense of the countless online interactions that take place. With a data-strong AI engine, Talkwalker has led the field of AI-based consumer research for more than seven years. All technological innovations were developed in-house, in order to be able to offer their customers the best platform for analysis of video, photo, text, and speech recognition.

An important project over the past few years was the Brand Love study, which took place in cooperation with Hootsuite. More than 1,500 international brands were analyzed in order to identify the 50 most popular. With the newly developed Brand-Love-Index, the three critical values for the development of love for a brand can be determined: passion, trust, and customer satisfaction. For the first time, tips that could be quickly implemented for increasing brand ratings complemented the study results. More than 2.6 billion conversations over social media, messages, blogs, and reviews were evaluated accordingly. "Priorities, values, and behavior patterns are subject to constant change. Only brands that are close to their customers can predict these changes and adapt in a timely manner. The brands manage to maintain the love for the brand and build on it," Elena Melnikova, Talkwalker CMO, described the Brand-Love-Report.

The study also demonstrated that customers pay close attention to the influence of brands on social, economic, and ecological developments. Many of the 50 top brands have therefore successfully increased their sustainability activities.

Fittingly, another large study was performed with "Shape Tomorrow." They analyzed customer reviews from more than 100 companies worldwide, and obtained a detailed perspective of their priorities, preferences, and expectations and were able to establish that in a good 54 percent of the cases, sustainability discussions conducted by customers were not noticed by the brands.

That is why the only companies that have a future are ones that fulfill their own expectations as well as the expectations of their users. The distance to the customer is decisive in adapting their strategy, message, and products to the changing expectations of the customers. Because if you understand what makes customers tick, and put the user at the center of your business strategy, you can make your company fit for the future. With Talkwalker, you have an experienced and reliable partner on your side.

FACTS AND FIGURES

PRODUCTS
consumer intelligence, social listening, social analytics, insight analyses and data storytelling

LOCATIONS
Luxembourg (headquarters), subsidiaries in France, Germany, United Kingdom, Italy, USA, Singapore, and Japan

FOUNDERS
Christophe Folschette and Thibaut Britz (2009, Luxemburg)

OWNERS
Christophe Folschette (Chief Strategy Officer), Marlin Equity Partners

EMPLOYEES
20 in Germany, approx. 600 worldwide

SALES
leading brands and agencies worldwide, data coverage in 187 languages

WEBSITE
talkwalker.com/de

TO WALK THROUGH THE TALK

Love Brands

❤ Deutschland, Österreich, Schweiz

1. L'Oréal
2. LEGO
3. Ducati
4. ASUS
5. Sennheiser
6. EnBW
7. Decathlon
8. Gucci
9. SAP
10. ROSSMANN

#BrandLove - Wie durch Nachhaltigkeit Markenliebe in der Gegenwart und für die Zukunft entsteht

X-PLAST

PRODUCT DEVELOPMENT FOR MEDI-
CAL TECHNOLOGY, THE TRANSPORTA-
TION SECTOR AS WELL AS
HIGH-QUALITY IOT DEVICES

Sustainable plastic from a 3D printer is
the specialty of the X-PLAST studio.
Counted among the customers of the
company are automotive groups and
manufacturers of medical technology.

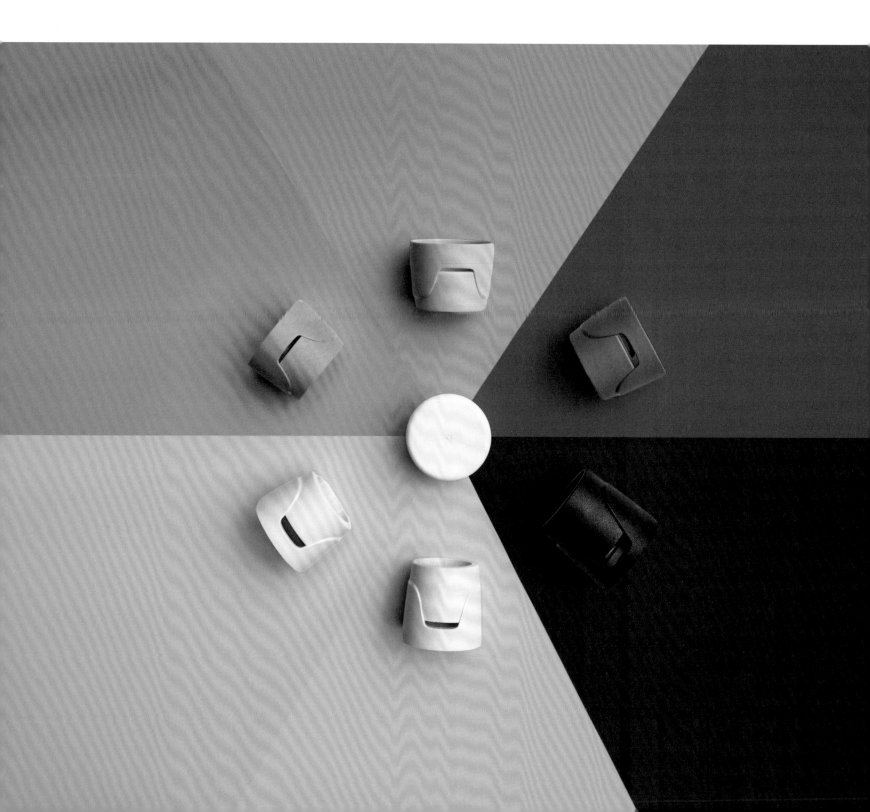

As a studio for product development with state-of-the-art equipment, X-PLAST has a goal of creating the best and most sustainable plastic products today for the world of tomorrow. The multi-award-winning team from Székesfehérvár, in Hungary, possesses a wide spectrum of expertise in the areas of design, development of components, simulation, 3D printing, and injection molding. Projects where the design team can test the limits of what is possible with plastics today in an environmentally friendly way are especially welcome. The in-depth technical knowledge about manufacturing possibilities and production differentiates X-PLAST from many other design studios, as reflected by numerous patents.

The company name stands for "eXcellence" at work with the material, "PLAST." Groundbreaking products for international clients are created through multidisciplinary teamwork among the young, flexible team of designers and engineers. The studio uses its knowledge to construct high-quality components for 3D printing, which are produced in-house along with prototypes and small-scale series. Their first large client, VW-Group, signed a contract with X-PLAST in 2016.

The year before, Viktor Seres and Zsuzsanne Galambos founded their design studio in Székesfehérvár with the idea to develop trendsetting products for medical technology, the transportation sector, as well as IoT devices for high-quality consumer products. At the same time, they have concentrated on plastics processing since the beginning. "Our goal is to find the best material to create a sustainable product with as little waste as possible," explained Viktor Seres. In their in-house 3D laboratory, X-PLAST offers state-of-the-art 3D printing with various technologies. Subcontractors are commissioned for the series production of injection molding projects, who are supervised by specialists from the team. X-PLAST supports its customers from their initial idea up to the implementation of the product.

The smart insulin pen cap "Indoo," which was developed by X-PLAST for the medical technology manufacturer Di-Care, won the German Design Award in 2022. The model transforms common insulin pens into intelligent devices. It is as comfortable to use as it is easy, and provides a contemporary style of diabetes data management in combination with an app.

In order to keep up with a constantly changing market, the Hungarian studio needs to be able to adapt to new situations while remaining true to its core values. As a small and highly-qualified team, X-PLAST is constantly evolving, through learning new technologies, skills, and software programs. Beyond that, the company offers training positions for future product designers. "Our main goals are to involve the entire team in understanding our internal needs and interpreting the needs of our customers," said Viktor Seres. "We can be successful together on the basis of these conversations."

FACTS AND FIGURES

PRODUCTS
product development for medical technology, the transportation sector, and high-quality intelligent devices with ISO certification

LOCATION
Székesfehérvár, Hungary

FOUNDERS
Viktor Seres and Zsuzsanna Galambos (2015, Székesfehérvár)

OWNERS
Viktor Seres and Zsuzsanna Galambos

EMPLOYEES
10 (2022)

SALES
worldwide, particularly in the EU and Switzerland

WEBSITE
xplast.hu

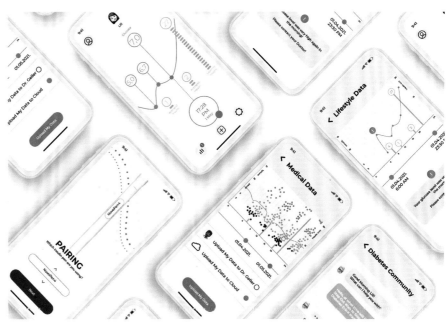

UP Designstudio

DESIGN

Product design is composed of more than the visual appearance of a product. With product design, experience design, and communication design, UP Designstudio unites usability, technology, and brand identity for product and user.

CABLE BOX

Today, it is no longer enough for a product to simply fulfill its function, if it wants to hold its ground against the competition. At the same time, design that is exclusively focused on the visual appearance can't make up for long-term defects in user friendliness. UP Designstudio supports clients during the development of products that create added value at the human interface through design and usability. that can hold their own during the interaction with the user. The holistic design of the user experience creates brand identities that generate enthusiasm purpose and ease of use, and aesthetics.

Well-known companies from the fields of industry, medicine, mobility, and lifestyle depend on UP Designstudio's power of observation and user understanding. With foresight, its staff uses creativity, technical interest, and design ability in order to combine the three design disciplines represented with the expertise of the client.

The result is that products are created that are gladly and sustainably used. During the design process, the expected users of the products are involved for exactly that reason. Their needs and requests are communicated during an evaluation process with interviews and tests, and create the central foundation for all further steps. That is how UP Designstudio creates the first sketches to the finished product series and translates technical complexity into clear brand messages.

UP Designstudio has been supporting its clients during the digital transformation. Even long-standing products need to have a digital layer added on. UP Designstudio uses its expertise in the area of communication design in order to orient the digital components of a product with the requests and usage habits of the client and to align them with the brand identity of the client in a way that makes sense, for example when designing a control interface or a web configurator.

UP Designstudio has proven their foresight with regards to the future of their own brand through their commitment to young designers. As a lecturer in the field of design as well as a member of the board of the Mia Seeger Foundation, Stefan Lippert, founder and managing director of UP Designstudio, is committed to the promotion of young talent. The young talent in the company is educated and encouraged through a comprehensive training program.

FACTS AND FIGURES

PRODUCTS
product design, experience design, communication design

LOCATION
Stuttgart

FOUNDER AND MANAGING DIRECTOR
Stefan Lippert (1994)

EMPLOYEES
33 (2022)

WEBSITE
updesignstudio.de

UP STANDS FOR USER & PRODUCT

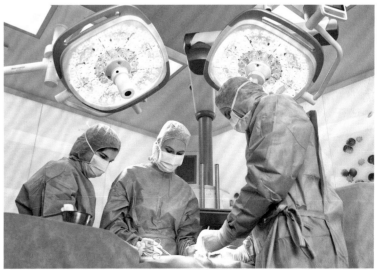

183

IBM iX

BUSINESS CONSULTING, EXPERIENCE DESIGN & COMMUNICATION, ENGINEERING & DEVELOPMENT, WORKFLOWS & OPERATIONS

As one of the largest leading digital agencies worldwide, IBM iX supports companies with their strategy, conception, implementation, and the operation of digital platforms as well as experience in the fields of innovation, marketing, sales, and service. The service spectrum encompasses everything from integrated omni-channel-communication, to work-flow optimization, to the development and incubation of digital ventures.

How does digitalization need to be designed today in order to inspire people tomorrow? IBM iX answers this question with, "holistic, sustainable, and user-oriented." The Experience Agency from IBM Consulting supports brands, companies, and institutions in their digital transformations: "We believe that good experience is good business. As a new kind of partner that has the size, industry knowledge, profound technical expertise, and appropriate methods as well as experienced employees, we can help to put the focus on the collaboration between people and technology," said Daniel Simon, Chief Design & Creative Officer and Managing Director at IBM iX. "Technology alone will not accomplish the systemic change that companies and society need today. What is needed instead are ideas, creativity, new ways of working, and one thing above all: people."

With scalable, flexible frameworks, like IBM Garage® and Enterprise Design Thinking, the digital experts at IBM iX work on sustainable business models, digital services, and integrated Customer Journeys. With IBM Garage®, customers collaborate side by side with IBM professionals. The method is well-founded, tested thousands of times, and refined. On the basis of IBM's consulting and technology expertise, which is tailored to the respective industry, successful value creation can be achieved quickly, and time and cost savings.

IBM Enterprise Design Thinking is a comprehensive toolbox of methods, with which challenges in digital business can be solved in a user-centered way. At the same time, human behavior is observed, understood, and reflected on, in order to approach the optimum design solution in an iterative and interdisciplinary way, as well as with empathy, excitement, and passion. "When positive interactions and genuine added value are created for people, then we're on the right track," said Marko Thorhauer, Experience Design & Mobile Leader IBM iX DACH.

Companies from different industries can profit from the sustainable approaches. That is how IBM iX achieves projects like the digital vaccination record, the CovPass-App, and a global D2C experience for the Swiss watch manufacturer TAG Heuer. With the HealthAdvisor, the digital agency has developed an AI-based app to prevent strokes. In addition, they created the new web presence of the brick manufacturer Wienerberger and the public transport company Berliner Verkehrsbetriebe (BVG).

FACTS AND FIGURES

PRODUCTS
business consulting, experience design & communication, engineering & development, workflows & operations

LOCATIONS
New York, London, Berlin, Düsseldorf, Ehningen, Erfurt, Hamburg, Munich, further locations in Austria, Croatia, and Switzerland

OWNER
IBM Consulting

EMPLOYEES
17,000 (2022)

SALES
worldwide

WEBSITE
ibmix.de

IBM iX

Robert Bosch

HOUSEHOLD APPLIANCES

The Bosch brand undoubtedly belongs to the pillars of the Federal Republic's economic success after the Second World War. Today, Bosch household appliances are in demand worldwide. Their design is as iconic as it is groundbreakingly innovative.

Still under the original brand name, Robert Bosch began his success story as a household appliance manufacturer in 1933 with the Bosch refrigerator. A few years later, the then barrel-shaped, 60-liter capacity appliance was followed by the Bosch Classic, a box-shaped appliance with characteristically rounded corners that remains a trendsetter in product design today. Even now the company hasn't yet tired itself out, continuing to set the standard with product innovations in functionality as well as design.

From the Bosch egg cooker to the electric toothbrush to the washing machine, dryer, or stove and oven- over the decades, Bosch household appliances have taken over a large portion of households in Germany — and increasingly worldwide — with its product guarantees of quality, reliability, and precision.

Even now, as a member of the BSH Hausgeräte GmbH brand network, the brand Bosch has remained an unchanged emblem of versatile household goods. The quality of the products has been independently verified time and time again, for example by the renowned Stiftung Warentest product testing foundation, and has secured the company's market leadership in Western Europe.

Bosch has always had the expectation of creating "technology for life." So, their product innovations remain aligned with the evolution of society and support it in its transformation. Whether it's the change in gender roles or even a modern understanding of quality of life and leisure activities: household appliances from Bosch support their users in shaping their daily lives according to their individual desires and as exemplified by the spirit of the time. With innovative new and further developments, Bosch also makes an important contribution to environmental protection and sets standards in the area of sustainability.

The Bosch design team works tirelessly on every newly developed product to create the design icons of tomorrow. The combination of different products, visual aspects, and functional qualities is demonstrated in the Accentline cooktop extractor fan. This forms a perfect synthesis with the Bosch induction cooktop. With the press of a button, an illuminated glass panel extends, which not only increases the extraction performance many times over, but also creates a pleasant atmosphere in the kitchen.

FACTS AND FIGURES

PRODUCTS
household appliances

LOCATIONS
40 production locations in Europe, Asia, Latin America, USA

FOUNDER
Robert Bosch (1886, Stuttgart)

EMPLOYEES
approx. 42,000 worldwide (2021)

SALES
specialty stores and retail stores, worldwide

WEBSITE
bosch.de

QUALITY, RELIABILITY & PRECISION

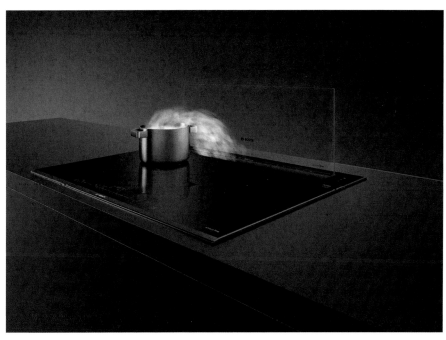

Well-designed products can fit into a wide variety of environments again and again over a long period of time.

LUTZ DIETZOLD

The German Design Council Foundation Members A–Z

3deluxe / design systems d.s. GmbH

A.S. Création Tapeten AG

AdHoc Entwicklung und Vertrieb GmbH

aed Verein zur Förderung von Architektur, Engineering und Design in Stuttgart e.V.

Aliseo GmbH

Amor GmbH

animaux Vertriebs GmbH

Architonic AG

Arno Arnold GmbH

ASA Selection GmbH

AUDI AG

avantgarde Acoustic Lautsprecher Systeme GmbH

AXENT Switzerland AG

B. Braun SE

BÄRO GmbH & Co. KG

Bauhaus-Archiv e.V. / Museum für Gestaltung

BAUR WohnFaszination GmbH

Bundesverband der Deutschen Industrie e. V. BDI

BDIA Bund Deutscher Innenarchitekten e.V.

Beatthechamp

Berker GmbH & Co.KG

Bethmann Bank AG

BETTE
Bette GmbH & Co. KG

bk Group
beyond the edge.
bk Group AG

BLANCO
Blanco GmbH + Co. KG

blomus
blomus GmbH

BMW Group

BORA
BORA Vertriebs GmbH & Co KG

BOSCH
Invented for life
Bosch Thermotechnik GmbH

BRAUN
Braun GmbH

Bretz
TRUE CHARACTERS
Bretz Wohnträume GmbH

brühl ☐
brühl & sipphold GmbH

BRUNE
BRUNE Sitzmöbel GmbH

B/S/H/
BSH Hausgeräte GmbH

bullmer
cutting room technology
bullmer GmbH

burkhardt leitner
modular spaces
burkhardt leitner modular spaces GmbH

BUSCH-JAEGER
Busch-Jaeger Elektro GmbH

BYOK
BYOK GmbH

CA GO
For all your precious cargo.
Ca Go Bike GmbH

C
Candela Lichtplanung GmbH
Candela GmbH

CANYON
Canyon Bicycles GmbH

carpetconcept
Carpet Concept Objekt Teppichboden GmbH

cloer
Cloer Elektrogeräte GmbH

CODE LAB
Global Mind Network

CONEL
CONNECTING ELEMENTS
CONEL GmbH

COR
COR Sitzmöbel Helmut Lübke GmbH & Co. KG

covestro
Covestro Deutschland AG

covestro
Covestro Polymers (China) Co., Ltd.

creative inneneinrichter
Creative Inneneinrichter GmbH & Co. KG

DART
D'art Design Gruppe GmbH

DALI
IN ADMIRATION OF MUSIC
DALI GmbH

DALLMER
Dallmer GmbH + Co. KG

dan pearlman
dan pearlman Group

DAUPHIN
Dauphin HumanDesign Group GmbH & Co. KG

DDC Deutscher Designer Club e.V.

DEDON
DEDON GmbH

Design Center
Baden-Württemberg

designaffairs GmbH

Designit Germany GmbH

deSter GmbH

Dethleffs
GmbH & Co. KG

Deutsche Bank AG

Deutsche Steinzeug
Cremer & Breuer AG

Deutsche Vermögensberatung
AG (DVAG)

Deutscher Designtag e.V.

DIHK

dormakaba International
Holding GmbH

Dornbracht GmbH & Co. KG

DRAENERT GmbH

Drägerwerk AG & Co. KGaA

Duncan McCauley GmbH und
Co.KG

DuPont de Nemours
(Deutschland) GmbH

DURABLE Hunke und Jochheim
GmbH & Co. KG

Duravit AG

DWD Concepts GmbH

e15 Design und
Distributions GmbH

echolot Werbeagentur GmbH

EDAG Engineering GmbH

EGGER Holzwerkstoffe
Wismar GmbH & Co.KG

ELO Stahlwaren
GmbH & Co. KG

EPAM Systems GmbH

ERCO GmbH

Erstes Deutsches Fernsehen

ET GLOBAL GmbH

evoq Deutschland GmbH

exitecture architekten
M.Hohl & F.Keller GbR

Factor Design GmbH & Co. KG

Felss Group GmbH

Festo Vertrieb GmbH & Co. KG

Fette Compacting GmbH

fischerwerke GmbH & Co. KG

Floating Homes GmbH

Verlag form GmbH & Co. KG

Foundry Berlin GmbH

FPS Fritze Wicke Seelig
Partnerschaftsgesellschaft von
Rechtsanwälten mbB

Freifrau Manufaktur GmbH

Frescolori.de GmbH

frogblue AG

FSB Franz Schneider Brakel
GmbH + Co

FUMA Hauszubehör GmbH

gantenhammer
GmbH & Co. KG

J.D. Geck GmbH

GEZE GmbH

Gira Giersiepen
GmbH & Co. KG

glaskoch
B. Koch jr. GmbH + Co. KG

Glen Dimplex
Deutschland GmbH

GMK Markenberatung
GmbH & Co. KG

Goldstein Studios GbR

Gebr. Graef
GmbH & Co. KG

GROHE AG

Hadi Teherani Architects
GmbH

HAFI Beschläge GmbH

HAGEDORN Management GmbH

Hailo-Werk, Rudolf Loh GmbH und Co. KG

Halbe-Rahmen GmbH

HANSA Armaturen GmbH

hansgrohe

Hansgrohe SE

HAWORTH

Haworth GmbH

Heithoff & Companie GmbH

HEWI

HEWI Heinrich Wilke GmbH

HEY-SIGN GmbH

HIRSCHMANN

Hirschmann Laborgeräte GmbH & Co. KG

HOLTZ OFFICE SUPPORT

HOLTZ OFFICE SUPPORT GmbH

Holzmedia

Holzmedia GmbH

HPP
Architekten

HPP Architekten GmbH

hund
MÖBELWERKE

Hund Möbelwerke GmbH & Co KG

hw.design gmbh

HYMER

Hymer GmbH & Co. KG

HYUNDAI

Hyundai Motor Europe Technical Center GmbH

IBMiX

IBM iX Berlin GmbH

iconmobile GmbH

ico

Iconstorm GmbH

ID AID

ID AID GMBH

IDZ International Design Center Berlin

IDZ | Internationales Design Zentrum Berlin e. V.

IHK Industrie- und Handelskammer Frankfurt am Main

IHK Industrie- und Handels-kammer Frankfurt am Main

IKA®

IKA Werke GmbH & CO. KG

IN medias Rees.
werbeagentur

In medias rees Werbeagentur

INDEED

Indeed Innovation GmbH

Interbrand

Interbrand GmbH

INTERNET STORES

Internetstores GmbH

interstuhl

Interstuhl Büromöbel GmbH & Co. KG

IPPOLITO FLEITZ

Ippolito Fleitz Group GmbH

jankurtz
*designed in affalterbach

Jan Kurtz GmbH

J. D. Schwimmbad-Bau + Design GmbH

J.F.S. Parfums Berlin GmbH & Co. KG

JOMOO

Jomoo Kitchen & Bath Deutschland GmbH

iJOY
lighting

Joy Lighting Co, Ltd

Albrecht Jung GmbH & Co.KG

JUNGvMATT
BRAND IDENTITY

Jung von Matt brand identity

JUNGHEINRICH

Jungheinrich AG

JUTEC
... immer eine Biegung voraus

JUTEC Biegesysteme GmbH & Co. KG

KERMI

Kermi GmbH

Kettnaker

Kettnaker GmbH & Co. KG

KEUCO

KEUCO GmbH & Co. KG

KFF®

KFF GmbH &Co.KG

kinema®

mykinema GmbH

KISKA.

KISKA GmbH

KLAFS
MY SAUNA AND SPA

Klafs GmbH & Co. KG

KLUDI
WATER IN PERFECTION

KLUDI GmbH & Co. KG

KNOBLAUCH
IDENTITY, HANDCRAFTED.

Konrad Knoblauch GmbH

Knorr-Bremse AG

koelnmesse

Koelnmesse GmbH

KÖNIG+NEURATH

König + Neurath AG

Koralle

Koralle Sanitärprodukte GmbH

KOLO

Kolo Studio

KOTOAKI ASANO
Architect & Associates

KOTOAKI ASANO Architect & Associates

KraussMaffei

KraussMaffei Technologies GmbH

KRUMPHOLZ®

Krumpholz-Werkzeuge e.K.

Küppersbusch FÜR KÜCHEN MIT STIL	**KURZ** 	KUSCH+CO	kymo	**LAMY** Design. Made in Germany.	ledxon	**LEICHT**
Küppersbusch Hausgeräte GmbH	LEONHARD KURZ Stiftung & Co. KG	Kusch + Co GmbH	kymo GmbH	C. Josef Lamy GmbH	ledxon GmbH	LEICHT Küchen AG
LIEBHERR	ligne roset	**LINKS DER ISAR**	loved		MARKGRAPH	markilux
Liebherr Hausgeräte GmbH	Roset Möbel GmbH	LINKS DER ISAR GmbH	Loved GmbH	Markenverband e.V.	Atelier Markgraph GmbH	markilux GmbH + Co. KG
martor	mauser möbel die mitdenken – seit 1896	mawa	MDLexpo	(m) MENTOR		MERCK
MARTOR KG	mauser einrichtungssysteme GmbH & Co. KG	mawa design Licht- und Wohnideen GmbH	MDL expo International GmbH	MENTOR GmbH & Co. Präzisions-Bauteile KG	Mercedes-Benz Group AG	Merck KGaA
 messe frankfurt	MEISTERlinie	MIA SEEGER STIFTUNG	**Miele**	mono	MÜHLE	müller möbelwerkstätten
Messe Frankfurt GmbH	MHG HEIZTECHNIK GmbH	Mia-Seeger-Stiftung	Miele & Cie. KG	Mono GmbH	H.-J. Müller GmbH & Co. KG	Müller Möbelwerkstätten GmbH
Naber	NEU GELB	NIEBERG | ARCHITECT	NILS HOLGER MOORMANN	nimbus[×]	**NOBLEX**®	**nolte** KÜCHEN
Naber GmbH	Neugelb Studios GmbH	Nieberg Architect	NILS HOLGER MOORMANN ART DIRECTION	Nimbus Group GmbH	Noblex GmbH	Nolte Küchen GmbH & Co. KG
NORKA	**NowyStyl**	NTT DaTa	**nurus**	Oase LIVING WATER	**OBJECT CARPET**	Occhio
Norka GmbH & Co.KG	NSG International GmbH	NTT DATA Deutschland GmbH	Nurus GmbH	OASE GmbH	OBJECT CARPET GmbH	Occhio GmbH
OLYMP® BEST SALON INSPIRATION	ORANIER	ottobock.	out nature by PreZero	oventrop	PAP STAR	**PARADOR**
OLYMP GmbH & Co. KG	ORANIER Heiztechnik GmbH	Ottobock SE & Co. KGaA	OutNature GmbH	Oventrop GmbH & Co. KG	PAPSTAR GmbH	Parador GmbH
PETER SCHMIDT GROUP	**PHOENIX**	**poggen pohl** 	**point** TEC	PORSCHE DESIGN	**PRENEW**	**PROLED**®
Peter Schmidt Group GmbH	Phoenix Design GmbH + Co. KG	Poggenpohl Manufacturing GmbH	POINTtec GmbH	Porsche Design GmbH - Studio F. A. Porsche	Prenew GmbH	MBN GmbH - PROLED

QLOCKTWO®	RAL COLOURS	rasch	rational®	raumplus®	RECARO	RECKLI®
QLOCKTWO Manufacture GmbH	RAL gGmbH	Tapetenfabrik Gebr. Rasch GmbH & Co.	rational einbauküchen solutions GmbH	raumplus Besitz-und Entwicklungs-GmbH & Co. KG	RECARO Holding GmbH	RECKLI GmbH
REGENT LIGHTING	reisenthel. keep it easy	RESOPAL®	RICHARD LAMPERT	RITTAL	ROLF BENZ	Ronnefeldt TEA EXCELLENCE SINCE 1823
Regent Beleuchtungskörper AG	Reisenthel Accessoires GmbH & Co. KG	Resopal GmbH	Richard Lampert GmbH & Co. KG	RITTAL GmbH & Co. KG	ROLF BENZ AG & Co. KG	J.T. Ronnefeldt KG
Rosenthal	RÖSLE SINCE 1888	RTL	ruf BETTEN Perfektion der Sinne	RZB LIGHTING	schlafgut®	SCHRAMM DIE BETTENMANUFAKTUR
Rosenthal GmbH	RÖSLE GmbH & Co KG	RTL Deutschland GmbH	RUF Betten GmbH	RZB Rudolf Zimmermann, Bamberg GmbH	Adam Matheis GmbH & Co. KG	SCHRAMM Werkstätten GmbH
schüller®	SCHULTE Lagertechnik	selux	serien .lighting	ProSiebenSat.1 Digital	SEVERIN Friends for Life	SHADESIGN®
Schüller Möbelwerk KG	Gebrüder Schulte GmbH & Co. KG	Selux GmbH	serien Raumleuchten GmbH	Seven.One Entertainment Group GmbH, ein Unternehmen der ProSiebenSat.1 Media SE	SEVERIN Elektrogeräte GmbH	SHADESIGN GmbH
SSS SIEDLE	SieMatic	SIEMENS	SimonsVoss technologies	SLOWLI concept	sonoro	spitzbart treppen®
S. Siedle & Söhne Telefon- und Telegrafenwerke OHG	SieMatic Möbelwerke GmbH & Co. KG	Siemens AG	SimonsVoss Technologies GmbH	SLOWLI concept	sonoro audio GmbH	spitzbart treppen gmbh
Steelcase	STEIN HANEL	STERN® OUTDOOR LIVING SINCE 1947	DEUTSCHES DESIGN MUSEUM	stilwerk	STUDIOWILLIAM	studiokurbos
Steelcase AG	Stein Hanel GmbH	Stern GmbH & Co. KG	Stiftung Deutsches Design Museum c/o Rat für Formgebung	stilwerk GmbH Hamburg	Studio William Welch Ltd	studiokurbos GmbH
STYLUS	Talkwalker	TECNOLUMEN®	T · ·	THE STORE DESIGN ERS®	TiCad® a perfect trolley	Tilia
Stylus Media Group Ltd.	Talkwalker GmbH	TECNOLUMEN® GmbH & Co.KG	Deutsche Telekom AG	The Store Designers	TiCad GmbH & Co. KG	Savaş Plastik San Ve Tic AS
Tojo™	TRILUX SIMPLIFY YOUR LIGHT.	trivida®	Ueberholz.	UP Designstudio	USM	VDID VERBAND DEUTSCHER INDUSTRIE DESIGNER
Tojo Möbel GmbH	TRILUX GmbH & Co. KG	P+L Innovations GmbH	Ueberholz GmbH	UP Designstudio	USM U. Schärer Söhne GmbH	VDID Verband Deutscher Industrie Designer e.V.

| VDM Verband der Deutschen Möbelindustrie e.V. | Vetter Pharma-Fertigung GmbH & Co. KG | Viasit Bürositzmöbel GmbH | Viessmann Werke GmbH & Co. KG | VIM Group Brand Implementation GmbH | Vincentz Network GmbH & Co. KG | Vitra AG |

     WALTER KNOLL

| VKI Verband der Keramischen Industrie e.V. | VOLA A/S | Volkswagen AG | Vorwerk & Co. KG | Wagner System GmbH | WALTER KNOLL AG & Co. KG | WAREMA Renkhoff SE |

    Wilkhahn

| Weidemann GmbH | Gerhard D. Wempe KG | Wenko Wenselaar GmbH & Co. KG | Deutscher Werkbund e.V. | WGSN Worth Global Style Network Limited | Wilkhahn, Wilkening + Hahne GmbH & Co. KG | WILO SE |

WINI MEIN BÜRO.   wodtke

| WINI Büromöbel | WINTER & COMPANY GmbH | wirDesign communication AG | WMF GmbH | wodtke GmbH | Wöhner GmbH & Co. KG | wolfcraft GmbH |

| Norbert Woll GmbH | X-Plast Ltd. | Carl Zeiss AG | ZVEI Zentralverband Elektrotechnik und Elektronikindustrie e.V. | Zwiesel Kristallglas AG |

INDIVIDUAL MEMBERS

Olaf Barski, Christoph Burkardt, Kai Ehlert, Prof. Dr. Gerdum Enders, Barbara Friedrich, Prof. Achim Heine, Jörg Heithoff, Albrecht Hotz, Armin Illion, Michael Knuf, Stephan Koziol, Prof. Stefan Lengyel, Prof. Hansjerg Maier-Aichen, Reiner Moll, Nils Holger Moormann, Christian Sieger, Prof. Dr. h.c. Erik Spiekermann, Eckhard Tischer, Roland Wagner, Prof. Dr. Othmar Wickenheiser

About the German Design Council

As the design and brand authority in Germany, the German Design Council has strengthened the social awareness of design worldwide since 1953. With the goal of promoting the design competence of German industries, and increasing the brand value of companies via a strategic use of design, the German Design Council provides a forum for communication and knowledge transfer with a broad spectrum of opportunities, as the leading center of excellence.

Membership

Strong brands need a strong design: only with this interaction can sustainable profits be achieved and new markets conquered. This conviction unites the members of the foundation of the German Design Council: the network consists of more than 350 companies from diverse industries that have recognized that design has a strategic factor of success. During various activities such as networking events, conferences, award ceremonies, and expert circles, the German Design Council Foundation connects members, design talents, and numerous international design and brand experts in order to promote the design discourse and deliver important stimuli for the global economy.

Design Talents

The transformation and innovation abilities of a company are more important today than ever before. A decisive motivating force for this evolution is young design talents. That is why the German Design Council has always seen one of their core missions as to not only promote the perspectives of students and graduates, but also to strengthen them in the public perception: the German Design Award Newcomer, the ein&zwanzig competition and the German Design Graduates offer them a platform in order to present their concepts and ideas for a sustainable economic, ecological, and socially aligned future, as well as the opportunity to make contact with leading people in the design oriented industry.

Communication and Knowledge

The foundation initiated by the German Design Council, the German Design Museum and its extensive library; the Institute for Design Research and Appliance (IfDRA); and the content platform ndion aim to share current knowledge related to the subjects of design, brand, and innovation, and therefore raise awareness about the importance of design. Whether as an interface and intermediary for theory and application-oriented practice, from industry-specific trend observations to in-depth design research, the German Design Council offers a top-notch range of services for imparting knowledge about relevant design topics through its numerous activities and initiatives.

The Internationally Renowned Awards from the German Design Council

Their internationally renowned awards distinguish the best companies, designers, brand strategists, and innovators in the world. Whether it's the German Design Award, the German Brand Award, the German Innovation Award, the ICONIC AWARDS, the ABC Award or others: here, great achievements are honored and brought to light. They are a valuable marketing instrument to position outstanding products even more successfully on the market. Awards ceremonies and exhibitions, as well as extensive press and communications provide an exclusive stage for the winners and put the spotlight on their best achievements.

The award ceremony of the German Design Award: the annual meeting place of the international design community... Credit: Manuel Debus

This site: Eva Marguerre and Marcel Besau: the shooting stars from 2014 are internationally in-demand today. Credit: Manuel Debus
Right site, up: Konstantin Grcic at the award ceremony for the German Design Award 2016. Credit: Manuel Debus
Right site, down: Hanne Willmann, German Design Award Newcomer finalist 2016. Credit: Thomas Koy

Die
großen deutschen
Marken
2020

Innovation.
Zukunft.
Gestalten.

Rat für Formgebung
German Design Council

Left site: Legendary designer Hartmut Esslinger, special guest at the Design Gala 2019, Credit: Christoph Hengelhaupt
This site: Presenting the book, "The Major German Brands," at the Design Gala 2021, Credit: Christoph Hengelhaupt

*A place for design knowledge and research:
the library of the German Design Council.
Credit: Christof Jakob*

The Presiding Committee

Professor Mike Richter
President
Dipl.-Ing. Nicole Srock.Stanley
Vice-President dan pearlman Markenarchitektur GmbH, CEO
Dr. Saskia Diehl
GMK Markenberatung GmbH & Co. KG, CEO
Dr. Petra-Karin Kiedaisch
Publisher, av edition, Member of the Board aed Verein zur Förderung von Architektur,
Engineering und Design in Stuttgart e. V.
Helene Menne
Commerzbank AG, Head of Group Communications
Kristina Walcker-Mayer
Nuri GmbH, CEO and CPO
Roland Heiler
CEO Studio F.A. Porsche, Managing Director Design Studio
Dr. Annemarie Jäggi
Bauhaus-Archiv e. V. Museum für Gestaltung, Director
Leo Lübke
COR Sitzmöbel, Helmut Lübke GmbH & Co. KG, Managing Partner
Philipp Mainzer
e15 Design und Distributions GmbH, Managing Partner and Creative Director
Caroline Seifert
Supervisory Board Commerzbank AG, Corporate Consultant for Transformation
Prof. Dr. h.c. Gorden Wagener
Daimler AG Mercedes Benz, Chief Design Officer

EXECUTIVE BOARD

Lutz Dietzold
Chief Executive Officer of the German Design Council

HONORARY MEMBERS

Prof. Dr. h.c. Dieter Rams
Prof. Herbert Hirche (deceased)
Prof. h.c. Dr. h.c. Peter Pfeiffer

Index

Good brand communication builds on content, is honest and authentic.

LUTZ DIETZOLD

Imprint

CALLWEY 1884

© 2022 Callwey GmbH / Rat für Formgebung Medien GmbH
Klenzestraße 36
80469 München
buch@callwey.de
Tel.: +49 89 8905080-0
www.callwey.de

We'll see you on Instagram:
www.instagram.com/callwey

ISBN 978-3-7667-2613-1
1. Edition 2022

Bibliographic Information from the German National Library
The German National Library lists this publication in the German National Bibliography; detailed bibliographic data is available on the Internet via <http://dnb.d-nb.de>.

THE PUBLISHER
As the design and brand authority in Germany, the German Design Council strengthens social awareness of design and supports companies in all aspects of their brand and design development. The German Design Council provides a forum for an interdisciplinary exchange of knowledge and ensures competitive advantages for its members: independent, experienced, international.

THIS BOOK WAS PRODUCED FOR YOU IN CALLWEY QUALITY:
We decided on a MagnoMatt in 150 g/m² for the inside pages of the book: a matte coated image printing paper. The coated, matte surface gives the contents a refined and high-quality appearance. The naturally speckled book cover fabric has a very high quality feel. TOILE OCEAN is woven from 100% recycled PET waste obtained from plastic bound in the sea. The cover is additionally finished with hot foil, UV varnish and a blind embossing. This book was printed and bound in Germany at optimal Media, Röbel/Müritz.

THE FOLLOWING PEOPLE HOPE THAT YOU ENJOY THIS BOOK:
Publisher: Lutz Dietzold, Rat für Formgebung/German Design Council
Project Leader German Design Council: Roland Pajunk
Project Leader Callwey: Anna Seidel
Project Management German Design Council: Fiona R.Radji and Steffen Lawetzki
Editing German Design Council: Alexandra Sender and Rebecca Espenschied
Company texts: Heike Edelmann, Judith Marnet, Florian Mittelmerten
Editing: Andreas Leinweber
Final corrections: Dr. Birigt Wüller
Design & layout Callwey: Sina Chakoh
Design German Design Council: Oliver Genzel and Armin Illion
Production Callwey: Dominique Scherzer
Translation: Lawetzki Translations
Product images: with the kind support of the participating companies

Liebevoll begleitet von